Challenge to Survival

By the same author

Samba
A Study of the Origins of Primitive Music
Man and Monkey

Challenge
to Survival

Leonard Williams

New York • NEW YORK UNIVERSITY PRESS • 1977

In the evolution of the primate line, an animal emerged that knew it was going to die. It wept, laughed, struggled with the forces of nature, fought for its children, and buried its dead with ceremony. It feared and appeased the unknown and made it into the known. It discovered the elements of art, science, and history, gave birth to the concept, and came face to face with itself. This book is dedicated to the survival of that divine and terrifying animal.

Contents

List of Illustrations

Foreword

In a world which contains three billion unit organisms belonging to the species *Homo sapiens* and in which we expect to put that number up to six billion by the year 2000, Leonard Williams represents one of those groups in danger of extinction —that of individuals, who have something they intend to be, do, think, write and with knowledge of what others are doing, not regardless, but despite this danger.

Williams's book *Challenge to Survival* contains much about monkeys, but it is really about man. Within the scientific field of animal behavioral studies there is a very long spectrum, ranging from those who argue that the scientists must regard the nonhuman animal (and even the human one, too) as an impenetrable "black box," into which you feed some input (specified in purely physicochemical terms) and out of which you record some output, described in similar terms, all the way to those who argue that in trying to understand how animals behave it is silly to neglect the clues provided by the best comprehended example we have of animal behavior, namely, that of ourselves and our fellow men.

Williams belongs far out toward the latter end of the spectrum. He has studied animal behavior by setting up and maintaining with astonishing success a breeding colony of lagothrix monkeys living in as natural conditions as can be arranged. He has then not so much observed them, notebook and tape recorder in hand (though he has done that, too) but rather lived with them, much as a social anthropologist lives with a society of headhunters in New Guinea or wherever.

The Harvard-Columbia-Cambridge trained anthropologist has to learn how to operate in the social behavior system of the headhunters, and we all recognize how illuminating have been the accounts by Ruth Benedict, Margaret Mead, Gregory Bateson, Bronislaw Malinowski, and others of what this learning amounted to. Williams is doing something similar across a broader gap, not simply from the Paleolithic to the post-industrial, but from the prehuman to the human. He covers vividly a fantastic amount of ground, from the wild primate to Hegel and Marx. Nobody can read this book without empathizing emotionally with something he was not reactive to before. Intellectually he will also have to reconsider any convictions he may have had about behavior, human or animal.

C. H. WADDINGTON
Institute of Animal Genetics,
University of Edinburgh

Acknowledgment

Photographs 11 and 12 are by Claude Lévi-Strauss and are reproduced with the courtesy of Allen Lane, The Penguin Press. All other photographs were taken by the author.

Introduction

It has been said that if the observer of animal behavior allows a personal philosophy to influence his interpretations he is likely to be subjective and unscientific in his approach. But with Strehlow's beloved Aranda aborigines in mind, the so-called subjective approach can also be taken as a natural disposition for interpretations that depend as much on imagination as they do on facts and analytical reason. In my view the value of interpretation rests no more on a choice between objectivity and subjectivity than it does on a choice between truth and the love of truth. More significantly, if—as I aim to show—the observer's own instinctual heritage or phylogeny is continuous with that of the animal he is observing, it will follow that his own insights and interpretations can be all the more enlightening because of it.

Many behavioral psychologists, however, claim that we must purge our subjective feelings and reason of all "human motivations," and analyze animal behavior strictly in terms of reactions to conditioning operators in the environment. To such an extent has this behavioral jargon influenced and corrupted language itself, almost everybody these days—even on a conversational level—speaks of reaction as though action itself were an obsolete noun. Clearly the dehumanizing behaviorist, who buries his intuition in a detached impartiality, will lose that sense of historical continuity with his natural heritage and with it a psychological predisposition for what is natural and objectively true.

The purpose of this book, however, is not simply to criticize the theories of official behaviorism. The project is more ambitious; it seeks to establish the moral dynamics of the nature of man and to define that nature and its origin in prehistory. The evidence for my conclusions has been taken from many fields of research, mainly ethology and anthropology, and from my own work in the study of wild primates. I have tried to relate this material to a philosophy of a self-realizing evolution, with the object of bridging the ever-widening gulf in our time between specialized research and historical synthesis, and also in the hope that it may help others, as it has me, to understand and meet the challenge to our survival that concerns us all.

Challenge to Survival

CHAPTER 1

The Innate Drive

I adopt a submissive attitude, with hand and arm shielding my face, and crawl toward him sideways, *tuff-tuffing* all the way. He is fifteen feet away, and I have a long way to go. If I am cautious and make no mistakes, the danger is relatively small. His powerful body is huddled and crouched in appeasement. I cannot see his face. He looks half his normal size ("I am not really so big"). Both arms and tail are wrapped around his head and face ("I will not attack you when we huddle"). Only a few feet away from him I can now see that his eyes are closed ("I trust you so much I will not even look at you"). I am now close enough to hear his teeth chattering ("Even my teeth are friendly"). I notice that his penis is erect. ("You may lick me when we huddle"). I draw confidence from the fact that the adult male never attacks while the penis is erect. I am now at his side with my forearm pressing against his. He croaks, *arrks*, sobs, and cheek-puffs, and quite suddenly he unfolds and puts one arm around my neck. The arm is raised high, and he pulls my face close to his armpit. I smell the pungent yet sweet scent in the long hairs of his chest. He is trembling, and I hear many little sounds I have never heard before. I croak and *arrk* with him in a mutual huddle and then make plans for withdrawing. This I must do very slowly and by facing him as I sit up. At the first sign of breaking contact all his emotive trembles and sounds cease. He goes not limp, but tense and rigid. As I sit up, he sits up. I give him a slight cut-off, mostly with the eyes, and crawl back with my head turned around toward him. If he chuckles for a play-fight, I shall depart from the scene quickly. To deter him I *eeoolk*, which conveys not only goodwill but also the desire for no contact. Slowly and

1

methodically he climbs the beam to the hatchway and goes out to the trees. I decide this is the last time I shall do it.

The foregoing description is taken from my notes on performing the friendship ceremony with a dominant-male monkey of the species *Lagothrix lagotricha*, or Jojo as he is known to me. Many behaviorists will tell you that such a monkey has neither a mind nor a will of his own, that all his appetites, desires, intentions, and moods are "responses stimulated by external releasers." In Queen's English this means that they are divined or brought forth by a mysterious entity called environment.

The official doctrine of behaviorism does not credit the animal with the ability to make its own decisions on whether it will or will not act, or on how it will behave in relation to its own disposition. On the question of who is the real initiator in the interaction between the individual and environment Jojo, however, has a simple philosophy: anything that goes on in the internal life of his colony or in his territory is his business. This may be little more than an article of instinctual faith, but it works. For example, three years ago Jojo initiated the appeasement ritual with me, but halfway through he changed his mind. He tore my hand, gored my head with his top canines, and chased me out of his territory. He had two wives and three children at the time, which made six "external releasers" in all if you include me. This so-called conditioned response to an "external stimulus" gave me good cause to believe that Jojo has a spontaneous and very effective will of his own, both for making peace and for fighting, and that his decision to make peace or to fight springs from his innate ability to act and not merely to react. That is my starting point for developing one of the main themes of this book, but to involve the reader more successfully I must consider the whole question in some detail.

In the last century zoologists were mainly concerned with the physical structure and species classification of animals, and their work relied almost entirely upon zoo and laboratory specimens. Dead or captive animals, however, tell us very little about the nature of animals in their own habitat, and real advance had to come from studying the living in a natural environment. Thus fieldwork became paramount, and with it came a new and vast knowledge on the behavior of animals in the wild state, in mating, territory defense, social grooming, and courtship ritual.

Fieldwork, however, is still the poor relation of laboratory research, which is to be expected in a technological society that puts computers before the humanities. Research in primate neurophysiology, experimental vivisection, and "intelligence tests" on the criteria of pulling levers or pushing buttons for food is more valuable for our citadels of official science than the study of motivational behavior in natural animal communities. A few research centers have set up captive "collections" in large enclosures with the object of studying their sociosexual behavior, but unless the confined areas are large enough to include elements of a natural life, the hierarchic structure of the group breaks down. Experiments in establishing zoo "colonies" have been so disastrous that the attempt has been abandoned. Zoos harbor "isolated" monkeys, or desocialized "mating pairs," false relationships that are alien to the basic sociality of all primates, monkey or human. Or they produce a degenerate collection of monkeys, never a true social group.

Throughout this book I shall draw upon numerous examples of natural behavior from our own colony of lagothrix monkeys. The objection can be raised that this colony is in semicaptive conditions and that its behavior will be modified by those conditions because they are to some extent artificial. The environmental conditions, however, bear no resemblance to those of captive monkeys in zoos and laboratories or to those of a pet monkey in the home. The colony has a defined territory that the monkeys will not leave and that they will defend against all intruders, and for the first time in the history of this particular species the group has established itself as a successful breeding colony in captivity. Nine infants have been born in the colony since the project began in 1961.

In the study of animal behavior today there are two main schools of thought: those who hold that the instinctual actions of animals are responses to environment, stimulated by "releasers," such as colors, sounds, and scents; and those who accept this concept but also hold that instinctual actions are nevertheless innate and spontaneous and may occur regardless of external stimulus. In other words, although the action-patterns of animals are stimulated by environment, these action-patterns are also motivated by phylogenetic impulses that are not mere automatic responses to releasers in the environment. Much of this new knowledge has shaken the foundations of official science and has given rise to a storm of abuse from the behaviorist school. Behaviorist doctrine has reached a most sophisticated form in the work of B. F. Skinner, who claims that motivational interpretation cannot provide us with a natural science theory of human and animal behavior. Skinner regards all animal behavior as under the control of selective pressures in the environment and believes that human communication also is based on a series of "stimulus response units."

If A meets B and says, "How are you?" Skinner asks us to interpret this as a first response by A to the stimulus of the "sight of B." Skinner would of course agree that the approach of A in the direction of B could be a response to a previous stimulus, such as crossing the street in order to avoid meeting someone else. It is significant for Skinner that we should not concern ourselves with metaphysical entities such as the "inner motivations" of the individual. But with the absence of a positive initiator the motivations of A and B are canceled out in the context of a "stimulus response" to each other. Each response is the stimulus of another. By going forward or backward in time on a help-yourself basis, the behaviorist is able to dispose of the whole problem of originality and initiation. We are all wandering about in a fairground, painting pictures, playing football, picking our noses, writing symphonies, studying animal behavior, and playing with our children, and it's all done by "external releasers" and "stimulus response units" triggered off by the ecology of the fairground and by our own "operant responses."

If responses on a conversational level occur "out of sequence" or seem to be unpredictable, Skinner calls them "intervening variables." The following I presume, since it is my own invention, would be an example:

HE: Where are you going?
SHE: Mind your own business.
HE: I apologize.
SHE: There's no need to. I was only testing your stimulus-response unit.

The strongest criticism of motivational theory by official behaviorists has been directed at the ethological concepts of Konrad Lorenz. Rejecting Lorenz's theory that certain forms of spontaneous behavior are not dependent on external stimulus, the ethologist John Hurrell Crook writes: "There is in fact no uncontroversial evidence that in the absence of stimulation, aggressiveness must find a spontaneous outlet."[1] Any fieldworker, however, who has made an interliving study with wild primates will know that a great deal of innate compulsive action characterizes the internal life of the group, particularly in mating, care of the young, and intraspecific aggression. In our own colony the female woolly monkeys during estrus display aggressively to the males. They begin with a posture of shoulder hunching, accompanied by a quick, gasping intake of breath and the lip-smacking sounds of invitation. They will also jump up and down aggressively, shake branches in the trees, and drag various objects across the ground with their tails. During these displays the female may turn and look straight at a particular male, repeating the sexual overtures of lip smacking, with shoulders hunched and elbows out.

In opposition to the case for innate spontaneous action, it can of course be argued that these displays are "elicited" by the presence of the males or by the unappeased desire to mate. This can lead to a highly sophisticated argument as to what operates first, the internal appetite or the external environment upon which this appetite depends. Actually, the dynamics of the interaction between a living animal (not an abstraction) and its environment (not an abstract ecology) cannot be defined in purely physiological terms, simply because the phenomenon itself is phylogenetic as well as social, self-determined as well as conditioned. In other words, a psycho-philosophical concept is required to do full justice to its objectivity. (This problem is taken up more fully in chapter 7.) Meanwhile, to make the case for innate and spontaneous action in animal behavior acceptable to behaviorists who stick to the party line, we would have to isolate the animal psyche from its own physiology, put it in a time-space vacuum, and if under these "conditions" it displayed some form of "spontaneous action," we would then have to meet the argument that the "behavior" was a response triggered off by the total absence of environmental stimulus!

In a woolly monkey ritual we call chest rubbing, displays of aggression and appeasement often combine in one pattern. The ritual in our colony is not restricted to the protection of territory; it is linked with many aspects of social and sexual behavior. The chest of the lagothrix monkey is where his body scent is strongest. For a baby monkey, who spends the first four weeks of its life clinging to the long fur of the mother's chest, it means security, food, warmth, and comfort. When he is old enough to make the acquaintance of other monkeys, it is the dominant males to whom he goes first, nestling down into their chests. Thus he learns the characteristic scents of individual monkeys and associates them with friendship and security. The infant becomes familiar not only with the scents of other monkeys, but also with the surrounding territory. With constant chest rubbing the males transfer to their chests all the scents of objects and places they have been to, so that the infants learn to associate them with home and security. The chest-rubbing display extends throughout the whole social and biological life of the group. Jojo and Ricky often greet each other with emotive cries, lifting their arms and exposing their chests, and then huddling close together while making the cheek-puffing sounds of friendship. These emotive sounds and gestures have distinct patterns and autonomous functions, but they often combine and overlap in sequences determined by changing moods and desires. Lip smacking, teeth chattering, cheek puffing, grooming, appeasement, and sexual overtures are accompanied by gestures and postures with roots in many impulses. Many of these highly expressive acts are so subtle and complex that they defy classification in terms of ritualized behavior. Their value for protecting the young and consolidating the group is clearly the function of social instincts that are inborn and not merely acquired by intimidation and group discipline. (Much is said about "appeasement ritual" in the social behavior of monkeys and apes that refers to nothing more than the expression of friendship. In a conflict situation one monkey may well express appeasement to another as a sign of withdrawal from the dispute, but the manner in which he conveys appeasement can also be used simply for greeting another monkey or expressing friendship. Monkeys have a considerable repertoire of gesture, posture, facial expression, and sound language to draw upon for communicating their feelings and desires to others. This communication system cannot be so neatly parceled up in the nomenclature of "ritualized behavior" and "specific action patterns.")

The most striking evidence I have received for innate phylogenetic movement has come from observation of the biological and social behavior of infant monkeys. I have been able to observe and study intimately the behavior of six infant monkeys in our colony from the moment of their birth to adolescence at the age of three. In all cases these tiny infants at the age of three weeks were making friendship overtures to other monkeys in the group and, most significantly, *by a head-shaking display that is peculiar only to infants*. This movement is also accompanied by appealing little emotive sounds of *tuff-tuff*. The head shaking and *tuff-tuff* sounds are unmistakably innate and spontaneous. They cannot be learned, because the adults and juveniles do not head shake or *tuff-tuff* in any of their friendship greetings or gestures of appeasement. Instead they crouch down, cover the head with the forearm, and cheek puff—a display we call "snuffling." Infant appeasement and friendship displays, besides being innate, also seek a spontaneous outlet. This is made very clear by the fact that infants will frequently act as initiators in their desire for new contacts, new experiences, and new relations with other members of the group. While on the mother's back an infant may reach out to another adult and evoke a "snuffles" response from that adult by head shaking and *tuff-tuffing*, sometimes even climbing off the mother and going for a ride on "father's" back.

The doctrinaire ethologist may reject my interpretation of this behavior on the grounds that infants may learn the head shaking and *tuff-tuffing* from other infants. In fact, when the woolly monkey Polly was born she was the only infant at the time in the colony, yet the display I have described was performed by her from the age of four weeks to one year, the stage when infant head shaking gradually evolves into an early form of juvenile "snuffling."

Innate phylogenetic movement is also humorously expressed in the behavior of the woolly monkey's prehensile tail, and there are many situations where such compulsive tail behavior requires no more stimulation than the simple fact of being alive. Our woolly monkey Samba, for example, had an amusing habit of describing erratic and tiny circular movements in the air with her hands, at the same time curling her tail up from behind so that she could hold and wiggle the end of it over her head. The performance took on a bizarre character when she stood on two legs and accompanied the act with an eccentric dance, alternating the roly-poly hand movements with tentative grabs at her tail. The behavior was usually a prelude to a high-spirited jump, where the slight element of risk always added to the excitement. In a downward leap she would maintain her grip on the end of the tail until she landed on the ground.

The compulsiveness of habitual behavior, like the child's innate obsession for detail, is also rooted in an instinctual reverence for a procedure already established rather than one that is unknown and invites the hazards of change. Should I begin a favorite story with my children: "Jack decided to join his brother in the woods, but before leaving the hut he put another log on the fire and locked the back door...," I am immediately corrected, as well as abused, with "*Wrong!* ... he put *two* logs on the fire, and he also shut the windows!"

An interesting example of how phylogenetic movement

combines with ritualization from habit has been demonstrated to me by the woolly monkey Jessy. Jessy and I often take a walk outside the monkey territory, trespassing on a neighbor's estate. All our monkeys are reluctant to venture into strange territory, but Jessy welcomes the opportunity of doing so in company with me. Ever since she was a juvenile I have held her tail when going on these excursions, not as a lead, but as the equivalent of "holding hands." Today, at the age of nine and with three babies to her credit, she will always lift her tail as she passes by, even when she has already made it clear by other intention signs that she has no desire to have her tail held and go for a walk. Should I in these circumstances grasp the uplifted tail, ignoring her cut-off gesture with the head, she is likely to give me an impression-bite for taking such a liberty. In short, Jessy's uplift of the tail, like the human gesture of lifting the hat, has become an autonomous acknowledgment of me whenever she passes by. To grasp her tail in these circumstances would be a breach of etiquette no less serious than to relieve a human passerby of his hat.

One of the most outstanding examples of animal initiative in relation to new types of behavior has come from the ten-year field study of a colony of Japanese monkeys on the island of Koshima off the coast of Japan. This project, which is continuing as I write, was begun in 1948 by Dr. K. Tokuda and Dr. J. Itani. It has accumulated a vast and exciting body of new data on the psychological and social behavior of the wild monkey group, including a detailed account of how the enterprise and initiative of one particular monkey led to a completely new form of social activity.

Friendly relations were established with the Koshima colony in the period from 1948 to 1953, during which time the monkeys were fed sweet potatoes. One particular monkey, a female named Imoko, picked up from the beach a sweet potato covered with sand and discovered by soaking it in sea water that the sand could be washed away. This custom spread throughout the colony, and within three years one-half of the monkey population had adopted the new culture of potato washing, which has since brought fame to Koshima.

The new culture spread first through kinship relations, from mothers to their children, until infants came to accept it as a social norm in the feeding behavior of the group. The culture is now established throughout the group and has become a part of its traditional heritage. A series of intelligence tests proved subsequently that Imoko, the originator of the culture, was the most enterprising and intelligent monkey in the troop. She was also the first to walk upright in water and to adopt the method of washing and brushing the sand away with her hands, while the remainder of the troop were still rolling the potatoes in shallow water to remove it. Intelligence and initiative varied among the individual monkeys, and those with the highest ratings quickly adopted Imoko's method of washing and brushing the sand away.

Imoko made another remarkable discovery—her preference for sweet potatoes that had been flavored or seasoned with sea water, with the result that she developed the technique of alternately eating the potato and dipping it into the sea water. Again the more intelligent members of the group followed suit. Imoko then instituted a new norm in the method of gathering wheat grain from the shore. The normal procedure had been to pick up the wheat grains painstakingly, one by one, and eat them. Imoko gathered the wheat and the sand together, scooped it up in her hands, and threw it into the water, thus separating the wheat from the sand in a method similar to that of panning gold. At this stage an antisocial element in the group began to assert itself. Some of the monkeys waited for the Imoko followers to throw the wheat grain into the water and then intimidated and drove them away in order to profit by their labor. These antisocial monkeys never acquired the wheat-washing technique. (This antisocial element in wild primate society is taken up again in chapter 5 as part of the evidence for a precursor of "immorality" in nature.)

It is clear that the initial exploratory acts of discovering new techniques can spread throughout the wild monkey group and become a social norm. This has happened in my own woolly monkey colony, mainly through the enterprise and higher intelligence of the woolly monkeys Samba, Jessy, and Jojo. Sir Alister Hardy writes:

It is adaptations which are due to the animal's behaviour, to its restless exploration of its surroundings, to its initiative, that distinguishes the main diverging lines of evolution; it is these dynamic qualities which led to the different roles of life that open up to a newly emerging group of animals . . . giving the lines of runners, climbers, burrowers, swimmers, and conquerors of the air.[2]

The orthodox behaviorist may argue that if Imoko had longer thighbones or thumbs that were more opposable, these would have been the result of random mutations that had already made possible Imoko's ability to discover new feeding techniques and to walk upright and carry food. This implies that all possible mutations are bound to occur in the course of time, each by chance, until one or more fortuitously turn up that are useful for new skills, and that these would be retained by natural selection because they served the interests of the species. In my view, this is as close as one can get to a theory of unnatural selection.

We know that the exploratory impulse to "discover" is already fixed in the behavior of the higher primates and does not have to be learned. From Goodall's field study in Tanzania we learn that chimpanzees in the wild use leaves like sponges, as drinking tools. This does not mean that the discovery of the usefulness of objects is accidental. It is the result of observation and recognition. The potto for example, like the monkey, is also a primate, and it is equipped with prehensile hands, opposable thumbs, and bifocal color vision. Now a potto may chance upon a cup in a domestic environment, but it will never discover the use of a cup, any more than it will discover the use of a leaf in its own habitat as a drinking tool. It may perhaps be persuaded or encouraged to use a cup, but this would not mean that the animal has the innate ability to initiate the act. The monkey, however, has inherited a long period of built-in experimenting and investigating and has a higher adaptive intelligence as an innovator. In our own colony all the monkeys are quick to discover the use of a cup by their own initiative. It can be said of the monkey that "opportunity makes the thief." In the case of the potto, however, such an "opportunity" is not recognized, even though this primate is equipped with the physiological machinery for picking up and drinking from a cup.

The significant factor in the development of the new behavior of the Koshima monkeys is that it was initiated by the enterprise of one particular monkey, Imoko. To regard accidental mutations and selective pressures as the determining factor in the rise of such behavior is equivalent to attributing the forty-eight fugues and preludes of Bach to the climate of seventeenth-century Protestant Germany and to the selective pressures of the clavichord, the organ, and the patronage of the German aristocracy. To say that "opportunities" and "limitations" imposed by selective pressures are the primary cause of movement and life is merely to emphasize the uncontested fact that we cannot sit down on a chair until an external culture has provided us with a chair, or that backsides must first evolve before they can be kicked. I at any rate prefer to think that Imoko and many other primates in our ancestry played a more dynamic part in lengthening our legs for dancing and developing our hands for making music than accidental mutations sanctified by natural selection. Natural selection does operate and random mutations do occur, but the dynamics of new behavior stem from the inner determination of living organisms to achieve the best results from the limitations imposed upon them. I shall return to the theory of "accidental-mutation-selection" in chapter 2, but first I must distinguish between two types of instinctual behavior, one ritualized and the other innovative.

A widely accepted view in behaviorist theory is that man has lost most of the autonomous motor impulses that give rise to the ritualized behavior of nonhuman animals and that this loss of "instinctual knowledge" has been replaced by acquired or learned knowledge. This has led to the theory that man has come to rely almost entirely upon the accumulation of traditional and cultural knowledge and that his instinctual life is withering away. The failure to distinguish between instinctual behavior that is highly individualized and the fixed action patterns of ritualized behavior has led to a great deal of confusion in ethological theory. Ashley Montagu makes the astonishing claim that man has virtually lost all his instincts: "In the course of human evolution the power of instinctual drives has withered away. . . . If there remains any residue of instincts in man, they are, possibly, the automatic reaction to a sudden loud noise, and in the remaining instance to a sudden withdrawal of support; for the rest man has no instincts."[3]

It is true that human behavior is less determined by fixed motor impulse, but only because it is more individualized and less ritualized, not because it is less instinctual. The unconscious mind is a phylogenetic reservoir of instinctual power and imagery. The creative urge itself is rooted in compulsive drives that push their way through to the conscious mind and to objectivity with the same relentlessness as the innate motor impulses that impel squirrels to jump and monkeys to climb.

A clear example of instinctual behavior that is unritualized (in the sense of fixed motor impulses) is found in the chant and dance ceremonies of tribal peoples. This instinctual and emotive behavior is culturally ritualized, and it is not comparable with the stereotyped ritual of compulsive behavior that we see, for example, in the territorial behavior of birds or the courtship ritual of fish. The pathogenic displays by chimpanzees when they hoot and stamp during a tropical rainstorm also express a highly individualized form of dramatic behavior. This too is similar to that of tribal man in his magico-ritual, when he dances and sings with the whole force of his being to appease the spirits and ensure his survival.

To regard new cultural knowledge as something that can be gained only by losing instinctual knowledge is to treat the subconscious levels of the mind as though they were an obstacle to new knowledge. Such negative reasoning denies the possibility of new emotions, new feelings, and perhaps even new instincts. It is said that because man has the advantage of a word language he does not have to posture like an animal, nor interpret the eye and the facial expressions of other men. It is true that instinctual communication by man is expressed far less in fixed action patterns than other animals, but this does not mean that men no longer communicate instinctually, that they no longer gesture, posture, and interpret the eye and face movements of others. So untrue is this that I give the smallest part of my attention to the words of the newcomer and all the rest to the stance and movements of his body, the expression on his face and in his eyes, and the tones and inflections in his voice; and I pray that he is doing the same with me, because in that way we shall both come to understand each other much faster and more reliably. If this is to be taken as a more instinctual and less civilized method of communication, then all I can say is the more uncivilized we become, the better. It is clear that all the confusion results from regarding instinctual behavior as the prerogative of nature, a kind of primitive backwater that we have inherited from our animal ancestors and the least acceptable from the parson's point of view.

Acquiring new knowledge does not mean that we lose our inherited nature; it means that we transform our nature into new modes of behavior and act and become more instinctually human, or humanly natural. There never was a monkey or a dog that could control its body, face, and eye muscles with the manipulative subtlety and range of expression that we find in a Marcel Marceau or a Charlie Chaplin. Man's natural ability and responses on his own instinctual level are a significant part of what is truly representative of human behavior. We are not merely talking machines. Man cannot flick his ears like a dog, use his toes like a monkey, or gyrate his neck like a goose, but neither have these animals the phylogenetic resources (never mind the fingers, hands, and brains) for expressing the sign language of the Iroquois Indians, or for hearing tonal patterns internally like a Bach, thinking internally like a Newton, or conceiving images like a Titian. And if we are so much richer in our instinctual resources than our animal ancestors, it is because we are standing on their shoulders.

Even our power to reason and analyze is rooted in what has been called the "curiosity instinct." Without the curiosity impulse the evolution of the intellect is inconceivable. It follows for me that the conceptual brain of man is not the "flower" of primate evolution. It is a new tool for developing a greater sense of moral responsibility that will meet new challenges to our survival. We have seen how the instinct for tolerance and responsibility works in the monkey community, and we have reason to be proud of our instinctual heritage. Let us be careful not to lose it, for there are those who prefer to see us as little bundles of conditioned reflexes, waiting, like Skinner's pigeons, for someone to turn on the light.

I therefore believe that man has inherited an instinctual social morality from his primate ancestors. Darwin comments on this:

There is no reason why man should not have retained from an extremely remote period some degree of instinctive love and sympathy for his fellows. . . . As man is a social animal it is almost certain that he would inherit a tendency to be faithful to his comrades, for these qualities are common to most social animals. As love, sympathy and self-command become strengthened he will feel himself impelled, apart from any transitory pleasure or pain, to certain lines of conduct. . . . He might then declare—I am the supreme judge of my own conduct, and in the words of Kant, I will not in my own person violate the dignity of humanity.[4]

In a later chapter I shall try to show that man is phylogenetically programmed for the culture into which he is born and that the human infant has in fact a built-in potential for acting morally. But there is much ground to be covered before the inborn nature of an animal in relation to its own culture can be examined in any depth.

CHAPTER 2

Design and Purpose

In the classical definition of Darwin's theory there are two main operators in the evolution of the animal and plant species: mutation and natural selection. The emergence of new species and changes in their structure and development are represented as the result of millions of years of random mutations retained by natural selection because of their survival value. The popularizing of Darwin's concept, the "struggle for existence," has since been taken out of the context of evolution as a whole and interpreted as though it were the dominating theme of evolution, as a ruthless war between the species.

There is of course fighting and conflict among the species, but predatory animals and their prey also influence each other to their mutual advantage in that selection pressures on certain functions and organs evoke corresponding adaptations. In the ecological balance of the total environment in nature the various species of plant and animal life depend upon each other for their existence, and the struggle between predator and prey is controlled by laws of preservation that protect the species as a whole.

Many animal species have become extinct in their failure to compete successfully with others who have evolved superior techniques for surviving. Techniques have nevertheless evolved for counterattack in both predator and prey, in the mobbing of predators by jackdaws, and in the claws of the cat. The survival value of interspecific aggression is all too clear, but aggression within the species, intraspecific aggression, appears superficially to be a form of self-destruction. It is in fact a species-preserving function as we shall see later.

Darwin was never committed to the proposition favored by so many of his followers: that inborn variations can arise only in the germ plasm and that acquired characteristics cannot be inherited. On the use and disuse of organs in the different animal species Darwin writes:

In many cases there is reason to believe that the lessened use of various organs has affected the corresponding parts in the offspring, but there is no evidence that this ever follows in the course of a single generation. It appears, as in the case of general or indefinite variability, that several generations must be subjected to changed habits for any appreciable results.[1]

Disregarding Darwin's warning, most of his followers concentrated on the main theme: that changes in the species occurred through accidental mutations favored by natural selection. In reply to this view C. H. Waddington writes:

To suppose that the evolution of the wonderfully adapted biological mechanisms has depended only on a selection out of a haphazard set of variations, each produced by blind chance, is like suggesting that if we went on throwing bricks together into heaps, we would eventually be able to choose ourselves the most desirable houses.[2]

To illustrate in some detail how one's reason can be outraged by the theory of biological change through selective pressures acting on random mutations, consider the following example: The woolly monkey in the South American jungle has evolved a special prehensile tail. Unlike the Old World monkeys in Africa and Asia, the woolly monkey's tail is an example of superb adaptation to a strictly arboreal life, determined by the unique character of the Amazon rain forests. Jojo's tail is thirty inches long and four inches in diameter at the base. It tapers consistently to its end, the underside of which is padded like an extra palm. Because of this prehensile end the tail has been called a hand-tail, but it would be more correct to describe the whole organ as an extra limb, which tapers down to one very sensitive and skillful "palm-finger." It is a most beautiful and remarkable organ.

Woolly monkeys can hang by the prehensile tail alone for long periods, and they use it for carrying as well as reaching for objects beyond the reach of their arms. Almost everything the elephant can do with his trunk the woolly monkey can manage with his tail. The prehensile end can even curl round and grasp a ball as firmly and securely as any hand; and when the owner moves along, up goes the tail in the air as though it had a life of its own and was resigned to going wherever the rest of the monkey chose to take it. While hanging from a beam with one arm, Jojo can pick up a kitchen chair with his tail and throw it at you. To appreciate the demands made upon one's sense of credibility when asked to apply the theory of "random-mutation-selection" to the evolution of Jojo's tail, we must now take a close look at some of the factors that gave rise to it.

It is generally accepted that the land mammals of the Old World crossed the Bering Strait during the Pleistocene, when there was a land bridge connecting east and west in the northern hemisphere. When the early primates went south to the neotropical forests they evolved into five-handed climbers, brachiators, and tail swingers. These early primates are divided into two main groups: pithecoids, which are "half" monkeys, and ceboids, which are "complete" monkeys. The common names of the species in the ceboid group are capuchin, howler, woolly, woolly spider, and spider monkey. The capuchins use their tails more than the monkeys of the Old World, but they have not evolved a prehensile tail; their thumbs are opposable, but not to the same extent as in species of the Old World. Looking for an evolutionary line within the ceboid group, I discovered that three organs in particular, the tail, the hand, and the foot, expressed a continuous process of biological change from one species to the next, strictly in the order of capuchin, howler, woolly, woolly spider, and spider monkey.

The closer I examined this development, the more astonishing and interesting it became. I noticed that the repetitive use of the tail not only expressed a structural and progressive de-

disposition for recognizing evolutionary design and purpose will be dismissed as "a subjective sentiment of no value for science." In place of our unscientific sentiment we are asked to believe that the development of the organs and behavioral characters we have considered (with full regard for the many changes accompanying them in additional bones, muscles, nerves, all of which combined and worked together as co-operative agents in a single purpose and in harmony with the phylogenetic drives of the particular species) was simply the result of accidental mutations favored by selection.

In search of evidence to test the alternative theory—that individual experience *does* affect heredity—the geneticists conducted a number of laboratory experiments on the fruit fly and the rat. By concentrating on isolated variations in eye color or removing the tails of generations of rats, they seemed to overlook the fact that a supreme factor in the transmission of acquired characters would have to be the repetition of stimulus acting on the use and/or disuse of various organs *in a total and natural environment.* Put simply, a "want" for change would have to be built into the instinctive machinery of the animal. This raises the old hoary question as to whether animals can transmit acquired characters of behavior and modifications of physique to their young, a theory commonly known as Lamarckism. Although recent laboratory research has come up with some new evidence that makes it necessary to reconsider the whole question, the objective evidence in nature for the inheritance of acquired characters was in fact provided by F. Wood Jones more than twenty-five years ago.

I believe Wood Jones was the first to draw attention to the analogous functions of the Chinese cashier and the modern geneticist. The Chinese cashier, flicking the little computer balls this way and that along the rods of his abacus, may be compared with the geneticist manipulating the little hypothetical balls called genes along the chromosome bars:

We now have a whole race of scientists trained in the refined use of the abacus of heredity. Their manipulation of the little balls of destiny has become an occupation demanding extraordinary skill and a great deal of specialized knowledge and literature. Beyond any doubt they possess an instrument and a technique that enables them to keep tally of the petty cash transactions of heredity. . . . I wonder at times if the great reliance placed upon the workings of the abacus of heredity is not the development of a higher mathematics of inheritance.[3]

One forms the impression when scanning the literature of contemporary research that Wood Jones's book *Habit and Heritage*, published in 1942, had never been written. It was Wood Jones who first drew attention to the fact that the squatting facets of the Indian Punjabis are also present in the Punjabi fetus: "The squatting facets on tibia and astragalus are present in all Asiatic peoples who adopt the hunkered position of rest, but they are absent in all people who know the habitual use of chairs." His book is well illustrated with drawings of the different squatting postures of oriental races and the Australian aborigines, the bone structures of leg and foot, and many other examples of specialized characters found in the Australian marsupials, all of which confirm the inheritance of acquired characters.

Today we know that individual experience does affect heredity, though not in the simple and direct way believed by Lamarck. Meanwhile, many geneticists are still ruled by the gene abacus, and the merest shadow of Lamarck's ghost is enough to inspire them with a new technique for calculating the hereditary factor in terms of natural selection acting on random mutations. But for many distinguished ethologists and biologists the evidence has already been provided by nature. Wood Jones writes:

Undoubtedly there is a higher sphere of inheritance, and it must be sought for not only through a microscope, nor by experiments carried on for a short time in the short life of one human being, but by a survey of what nature, with unlimited time at her disposal, has effected among living things.[4]

Evolution works neither by blind chance nor predetermined plan. In the dialectic of evolution "mistakes," "experiments," "blind alleys," and "retreats" must all be recognized as necessary steps in the relentless struggle for finding new ways of perfecting and stabilizing the species. Ludwig von Bertalanffy writes:

While fully appreciating modern selection theory, we nevertheless arrive at an essentially different view of evolution. It appears to be not a series of accidents, the course of which is determined only by the change of environments during earth history and the resulting struggle for existence, but is governed by definite laws, and we believe that the discovery of those laws constitutes one of the most important tasks of the future.[5]

Evolutionary "dead ends" are represented by those species that have become stabilized and can advance no further, with the result that they always run the risk of overspecialization and extinction. The two-toed South American sloth, for example, has hooklike claws, no trace of a palm, black enamelless teeth, and only six bones in its neck instead of the normal seven. Its fur, instead of falling from the backbone to the stomach as in other animals, grows along its belly and flows up toward the spine. This fur supports a growth of microscopic green-tinged plant life or fungi. Without a branch to cling to, the animal has the greatest difficulty in moving at all. As a perfect adaptation to an upside-down life in the Amazon forests, the sloth is an excellent example of what has been called an evolutionary dead end.

Evolution, however, by a process of rejuvenation known as paedomorphosis, is able to retrace its steps and make a fresh start. This it did at the frontiers between the insectivores and the tree shrews, which gave rise to the primate line, from the genus *Pupaia* (various forms of tree shrews) to *Homo sapiens*. In this way evolution is able to despecialize. By returning to an earlier stage, it begins a new line by allowing the infantile characters of a more primitive species to continue developing beyond the stage of sexual maturity. This is accomplished by a change called neoteny, by which infantile traits in the fetus are retained and allowed to develop into adult life. Many species of flightless birds, such as emus and penguins, are examples of neoteny. At a late stage of fetal development the down that covers the chick at birth is retained. This infantile trait is then developed and carried over into adult life.

It is clear that we must distinguish between a specific "error" and the concept of evolution as a creative process. The arthropods, for example, were faced by the problem of brain growth at the cost of constricting the alimentary canal or food channel. An increase of consumption meant the loss of intelligence for capturing food, and an increase of intelligence meant losing the food channel, with the prospects of death from starvation. Wood Jones gives an example of this evolutionary dilemma in brain building among the invertebrates: "Phylogenetic senility comes with the specialization of blood sucking. . . . The invertebrates made a fatal mistake when they started to build brains around the oesophagus. Their attempt to develop big brains was a failure and another start had to be made."[6] The evolutionary solution to this dilemma, however, cannot be interpreted as an accident or a mistake. Although biological concepts are not supposed to disclose the historical significance of evolutionary continuity, this has not prevented the official voice of behaviorism from declaring all evolutionary "mistakes" to be unqualified failures. In this way the doctrinaire evolutionist protects his "scientific impartiality" by opposing the concept of a self-regulating evolution with his own metaphysic of accidentalism.

A passive interpretation of evolutionary "error" overlooks both the persistence with which evolution achieves its purpose and that a process of trial and error is itself a method, not random behavior. One may, for example, learn nothing from one's mistakes and continue to work blindly until a way is found by accident. Another method is to profit by the experience of acting progressively and persistently in a number of directions until a way is found that advances beyond all the others. A creative entity, whether as evolution, a scientist, or an artist, does not begin with a preconceived plan. If it began with absolute knowledge of its goal, its work would be neither original nor creative; everything would be predetermined and carried out according to a fixed plan. In such a despotic evolution there could be no enterprise or discovery, no freedom as the right of self-determination.

Evolution works in much the same way as an image in the mind of a creative thinker. The image is experienced as an inner need, but labor is necessary to give it objective form. A composer will have an irrepressible urge to write a symphony, but he may explore many avenues before the imagery in his mind reaches a final shape in the creative act. And should he feel that the end result is wanting, or even a failure, he may begin all over again in his determination to make the objective form correspond with his image. He is driven by an inner need to try to perfect his image and endow it with life in the physical world.

CHAPTER 3

To Humanize or Not

The ground I have covered so far has made one thing very clear: the motivational behavior of animals is subject to the same evolutionary laws of growth, design, and purpose as those that operate in the human mind. It follows that the human observer's own instincts or phylogeny must be continuous with that of the animal he is observing and that his own motivations and power of reasoning will also be rooted in those instincts. This does not mean that the motivations of monkeys and men are identical. It means that because the monkey and the ape are our closest zoological relatives, they are bound to exhibit characters similar to our own, and that any interpretation of those characters in comparative studies must inevitably receive a *human* definition.

To humanize does not mean that we should treat monkeys as though they were backward editions of ourselves. Nor does it refer to a "pet" relationship, in which the owner treats the animal as though it were a human being. There is, however, a great deal to be learned about the internal life of the monkey colony by trying to relate and communicate with individual monkeys on their own instinctual level, provided the animals have a natural and independent way of life.

The relationship between the monkeys and the humans in our own sanctuary expresses a social mutuality that breaks through the barriers of species and territories, enriching the way of life of both. The friendship and mutual trust that develops as a result of personal contact on a social level yields a particular kind of knowledge, one that cannot be acquired through the bars of a cage or by impersonal field studies in the wild. It belongs to a dimension that cannot be experienced by the laboratory worker who is faced by a row of cages or by the curator who makes his daily round of the zoo and shakes hands regularly with the orangutan. To understand a monkey, one must to some extent be accepted as a monkey when one learns what it feels like to be a monkey. Most rewarding is the thrill of being accepted as a friend to a *wild* baby monkey with the approval of its mother and to win from the mother the trust that she extends to members of her own community. Such a friendship has not the remotest connection with a "pet" relationship or with that of a human foster mother to a de-socialized orphan monkey that has to be fed from a bottle as a substitute for a natural mother. The point is well made by Erik Erikson:

One can study the nature of animals by doing something *to* them, but one can really learn something about the essential nature of living beings only by doing something *with* them or *for* them. . . . One remembers here the work of Konrad Lorenz, and the kind of interliving research which he and others have developed, making the animals part of the same environment in which the observer lives his own life cycle, studying his own role as well as theirs and taking his chances with what his ingenuity can discern.[1]

The knowledge acquired from fieldwork is of course no less valuable than the special insight that depends on personal involvement. The observer will see much that is missed by the participant, no matter how much the latter is able to experience what the observer can only see. The participant, however, is likely to bring back with him some vivid impressions that cannot be known to the observer, though he must rely on his memory for describing them. The complementary advantages of both methods are made very clear in the following examples.

When the female monkey Lulu in our colony had her first baby, the mature and dominant males treated her with even more respect, displaying a great concern for the well-being of both mother and baby. Lulu had always been a formidable proposition for the juvenile males to counter because of her high rank, her age, size, and strength. But with the arrival of the baby they assumed that she would be more approachable. They were mistaken. She tolerated their interest in the new baby up to a point, but the self-assertive adolescent who took too many liberties was likely to receive a sharp lesson in the social disciplines of a dominance hierarchy. When her good nature was strained beyond the breaking point, Lulu would scream and tail-grip the leg or tail of the juvenile male, holding him tight, and sometimes scaring him out of his wits. Nothing used to please me more than to see young, pugnacious Jimmy, his adolescent dignity all at sea, held in a grip of iron by Lulu, both peering round at each other with their tails interlocked, and Jimmy screaming to his ancestors for help. In this situation it was Lulu who decided how and when a dispute must end. Such observations teach us a great deal about dominance behavior in the social life of the monkey colony, but the knowledge that comes by direct contact and personal involvement is equally valuable.

By personal involvement one encounters certain elements of behavior that cannot be felt, heard, or seen even by the most competent of trained observers. The difficulties are of course obvious, as I learned to my cost in performing the friendship ceremony with Jojo. But there are many ways that are less dangerous, such as play-fighting with a juvenile male. Only by inflicting a deciding bite (an impression bite that does not puncture the skin) in rough play with a juvenile male can the victor appreciate the full significance of the ear-splitting screams of rage and frustration that come from his opponent. The human participant is not acting cruelly; healthy aggression contests in the monkey group are quite natural and must not be confused with pathological aggression. These screams are not merely a prelude to submission or a warning sound that inhibits the victor. They are also a weapon of physical defense, a terrible weapon, for if you suffer it within a few inches of your ear you will go temporarily deaf in that ear. The victor is compelled to release his hold and turn his head away.

The following incident is typical of a woolly monkey in a domestic situation: Jessy, together with her baby Tina, has just arrived in the lounge and made herself comfortable in an easy chair. She has spent most of the morning in the trees with Tina on her back, and she is not feeling particularly energetic. I enter several minutes later and sit down some distance away from her. I do not greet her, and I make no sign that I am even aware of her presence. I know that she is looking at me and that she would like me to go over and say hello. Her instincts tell her that it is up to the male to make the overtures of friendship. Eventually she comes across and sits beside me, takes the tobacco tin out of my pocket, opens it, and helps herself to the cigarette papers. Each paper is ceremoniously pulled out, chewed, and dropped onto my lap. If in despair I should put the book down and say, "Jessy, you're a very naughty girl," she collapses into another snuffle and waits for reassurance. When I whisper and chuckle in her ear, her eyes sparkle and she shows her teeth. She then play-bites me on the nose, takes off my glasses, and drops them onto the floor. The subtlety and emotional level of this kind of behavior cannot be measured simply in terms of intelligence. It is a clear example of the humanlike character of a woolly monkey.

It would seem that the main concern of the impartial observer is to establish a terminology that will describe specific patterns of behavior as though human reason itself were an obstacle to truth. One zoologist cautions us: "Monkeys and apes are so closely related to the human animal that the dangers of anthropomorphism are constantly present. This 'humanizing' can be deliberate or accidental. Accidental 'humanizing' of primate activities can distort objectivity in a subtle way." A more profound warning, aimed at the dehumanizing zoologist, comes from Konrad Lorenz: "With close relatives such as monkeys we must expect to find characters which are inherited from common ancestry by them and by us. The similarity is not only functional but historical, and it would be an actual fallacy not to humanize."

We must of course distinguish between the species-preserving skills of an animal, such as the beaver's autonomous instinct to build a dam, and an animal's ability to learn new techniques, act creatively, and communicate on a more developed psychological level. But if we were to expel all the so-called prejudices of humanizing from our interpretations of wild primate behavior *on that level*, an appraisal of the *emotive* behavior of the higher primates would be impossible. In this context scientific humanizing may be defined as an interpretation that is all the more enlightening because it recognizes an instinctual continuity and empathy with the animal it seeks to understand. Such interpretation will also be more alert to the unique differences between the species as well as their similarities.

The disinfected concepts of the dehumanizer would have little value in tribal society, where a profound zoological knowledge is necessary for economic survival. There are many descriptions in the lore and song of tribal man that display an astonishing combination of accurate reporting and observation. The preciseness of many such descriptions comes from the observations of the hunter. The following song gives the names of the trees frequented by the monkey, the fruit he eats, a description of his movements, and it expresses the human standard of measurement (which the dehumanizer would no doubt call "the subjective naivete of the primitive mind") in a most dramatic and discerning way:

> Proudly he walks up and down,
> from bough to bough he skips
> on the anag-tree, the monkey.
> In his cheek-pouches he sticks
> the sweet fruit of the manow.
> Father, mother, look at him.
> He peers into the distance,
> he sees the bateg'n fruit,
> he grinds them in his fists.
> "You, give them to your father"
> his mother shrieks in warning.[2]

The native does not need to be excused on the grounds that it is natural for him to anthropomorphize because monkeys resemble men in so many ways. When the hunter expresses the motives of monkeys in human terms he adds to his understanding of them. (The botanical and zoological knowledge of the savage, which is no less orderly than that of the most exacting taxonomist, is considered in some detail in chapter 9.) With the handicap of what the jazz musician would call a "tin ear," it is to be expected that a great deal of primate research into the vocalizing of wild primates is likely to be "off key." I am not suggesting that the primatologist should climb into the trees with a tuning fork, but I am suggesting that very little will be learned about the language and communications systems of wild primates by standing under a tree with a notebook in one hand and a tape recorder in the other. The vocal repertoire of the South American monkeys is rich and varied in meaning, but apart from the more obvious call-cries and distress sounds, it cannot be usefully interpreted when divorced from expressive forms of posture and gesture by which it is qualified and always allied. Vocalizing must also be related to a given situation within the group, which is exceedingly difficult to do, if not impossible, in close canopy jungle such as we find in the Amazon area.

A species living in close canopy swamp jungle, such as we find in the interior of Malaya and the Amazon region, must rely on a wider range of vocal communication than required by a species living in open terrain, savannah, or in rocky mountainous regions, where communication by posture and sign can be easily seen. This no doubt accounts for the prodigious vocalizing and tonal range of the "singing" gibbons in the Malayan jungles and the awe-inspiring vocalizing of the howler monkeys (Alouatta) in the South American equatorial forests. The following extract has been taken from my notes on the vocalizing of lagothrix monkeys:

Trilling, which can best be expressed as *Eeeeooolk* . . . , is usually a long-distance call, and it can be heard only in the tree area of the colony territory. It has many variants of less intensity, which express greeting or simple pleasure. The long-distance trill-call opens with an explosive and long *Eeeeooo* . . . into a crescendo and then descends with a trilling glissando into . . . *ooolk*. It is a strong and most beautiful sound, and sometimes very sad and plaintive. In general it means "All is well." But should Jojo discover that one of the juvenile monkeys is missing, his call-cries will express the anxiety he feels because of their absence. The change in the quality of the sound is incredible. It opens with the strength of the "All is well" cry, but halfway through, at the point where it descends in a trilling glissando, it takes on a quality of melancholy, almost of anguish. Unlike trilling, all forms of barking and cough-grunts are aggressive in character. They are made at the back of the throat with the mouth wide open and teeth exposed. There is a particular cough-bark that is extremely dangerous in meaning for the intruder. It contains elements of both fear and aggression, of a fear that is being conquered by a sense of injustice and extreme rage, and therefore by a monkey who is ready to fight. If he is a dominant male he will stand his ground, though he may turn his head to imply, "I do not wish to carry this any further." Should a juvenile monkey evoke the sound from a dominant male (which happens rarely), he will either run away or make the submissive gesture of covering the face and "sobbing." In this situation the gesture is usually accepted as an apology.

There is one aggressive warning sound that is rarely used, an explosive cough-bark of tremendous volume. The strongest bark from our wolfhound Tim does not compare with it. It is the most dangerous of all sounds for the intruder, a sound of great and profound anger on the part of the dominant males. I have never heard the females use it. It comes deep from the chest, yet is so short and strong that it seems to echo everywhere at once. Unlike the ordinary screams of defiance, rage, and intimidation, this sound is not irrational or enraged; it is an aggression sound of tremendous strength, deliberation, and calculated design, used only as a long-distance danger call. I have heard it only on three or four occasions in all the years I have known woolly monkeys. Coming from Jojo, it is indeed a frightening sound.

Jojo today is an adult male, sexually mature, and the leader of the colony. His natural affections and responsibilities are now fully occupied with maintaining order and stability in his own colony with the result that he now regards any social fraternizing between me and the other monkeys as an interference with the internal life of the group. However, there are still occasions when Jojo, in his own humanlike way, will remind me that we once had a very close friendship. For example, the monkeys and I have a ritual of sharing a packet of cigarette papers. It is the nearest we can get to a social smoke. We form a group, and each primate takes a cigarette paper, chews it, and spits it to the ground. The ceremony is performed in absolute silence and solemnity. Jojo used to enjoy this innocent and simple little ceremony of goodwill until the advent of his puberty and the sudden realization that I was not a true friend, but a rival, and an outsider at that. It is too dangerous these days to perform the ceremony in any of the monkey houses. It has to be done in the monkey enclosures where there are plenty of escape routes (for me). On these occasions Jojo watches from a distance, usually in the hatchway at the end of the corridor leading into the monkey house. I am reasonably safe, because if he changed his mind it would take him a full six seconds to reach me. Within recent times Django has also left our circle, and he too watches from a distance. Magnificent Jojo, however, sitting there so dignified and aloof, is a sad subject for me to contemplate. When the ceremony is over, I leave the enclosure and approach him on the outside of the corridor cage. I offer him a whole packet of papers to himself for old time's sake. With his head held high and without looking at me, he takes the packet, pulls out a few papers, and has a little chew all on his own. He makes the deep-throated pleasure-sound of *eeolk*, but he turns his back on me every time I speak to him. Jojo is pleased, but he is quite definitely not going to show it. He is only human after all.

CHAPTER 4

Aggression

In the dominance hierarchy of the woolly monkey group there is always a leader, but really serious fighting for leadership is rare. Conflicts and disputes are usually resolved by appeasement. Nevertheless, intraspecific aggression plays its part in stabilizing the social code. Without it the internal life of the group would be chaotic.

A play-fight between a juvenile and a dominant male can begin with the best of intentions, yet still go astray, especially from the juvenile's point of view! The dominant male, for example, may decide to build up confidence in the young male by feigning defeat and running away to encourage the young male to chase him. For the observer, the impression given is that the dominant male has had second thoughts about continuing. Should the juvenile, however, throw himself into the chase with too much confidence and aggression, he may find himself landing right into the arms of a chuckling adult, whose eyes twinkle wickedly with amiable triumph as he turns around unexpectedly to catch him. The young male may then receive the roughest treatment he has ever had in his life, but the experience is also a lesson in aggression strategy he is unlikely to forget.

The extreme importance of a healthy and stabilized ranking system is clear. Until this evolves, fighting and violence, as distinct from protective and disciplinary aggression, is inevitable. In the daily play-fighting between all members of the group, every aspect of the opponent is explored and understood. These contests take on the character of rivalry in sport, in that relationships are established honestly and the order of social rank founded upon personal merit.

A false interpretation of natural aggression has come from those who claim that the primary social urge of both man and ape is to climb the social ladder and that all fraternizing and appeasing by leader males is a form of placation for maintaining power. In our woolly monkey group the dominant males are extremely affectionate to all juveniles as well as to the females and infants. Only when the young males take too many liberties are they likely to be disciplined by the adults. On one occasion I witnessed a most remarkable demonstration of an innate sense of social responsibility in the behavior of Jojo. It occurred when the colony was first given access to a tree area that had been added to the monkey territory. On that day we had expected all the monkeys to go running across the ropes to the trees. Instead, only Jojo went and he went alone. We have since referred to the incident as "the day Jojo tested the trees." When he sped across the ropes to the first tree, he paused on a high branch and peered in all directions. There was no swinging, leaping, or running. A swinging action was used only when he hung by the tail to test the lower branches with his hands. Deadwood and old branches were broken off and dropped to the ground. Gradually his passage through the trees expressed a definite pattern. Alternative routes were examined with caution until, stage by stage, he learned the whole tree area. For two days a small group of beech trees was investigated in this way, and not one monkey in the group was allowed to share in the exercise. Whenever the young males tried to join him, they were chased back to the tree platform and down the ropes to the enclosures and the indoor houses. A female named Jessy (who has since had five babies in the colony) was an adolescent at the time, and it was she who made the first and most successful attempt to reach the trees without interception. She cascaded through the branches with gay abandon, swinging and leaping, fortunately without mishap, even though a lot of deadwood cracked under her weight. Jojo was enraged. He rushed across with mighty leaps and chased her back to the tree platform. When he finally caught her he seized her by the shoulders and gave her a severe shaking. Not until the third day of tree testing was the group as a whole allowed the freedom of the new tree area.

This incident shows that the real significance of natural male dominance lies in the responsibility to protect the group, particularly the females and infants. Until the dominant male can control all those he is to protect, he cannot function as a respected and responsible leader. Dominance, therefore, is not domination. A pathological dominance takes over in zoo "colonies," where kinship ties cannot be nurtured in a confined space and where overcrowding leads to social tension and fighting among rival males. Brutality becomes the determining factor in establishing rank, with the result that leadership falls to despots with no real sense or experience of social responsibility.

When the so-called struggle for dominance in nature is placed in its proper context we see the danger of comparing it with the "status drive" of the human male in the "human zoo." The analogy overinterprets dominance-aggression and sexual rivalry among wild primates and fails to recognize that mutual tolerance prevails among dominant males in chimpanzee and gorilla groups, even when the females are in estrus.

The behavioral plot thickens when the stress experienced by our "human leaders" is compared with the status tension suffered by baboon despots in the desocialized environment of the zoo. A true parallel will compare the dominant capitalists who control our "human zoo" with the superstatus zoo proprietors who play their part in alienating baboons from their natural culture and putting them in prisons called zoos. Like the owners of the animal zoo, the dominant capitalists in the human zoo live "outside," enjoying a relatively remote affluence at "the top." The monkey despot, however, in the animal zoo suffers the same stress as the oppressed animals he dominates. In common with his tyrannized subjects he too is the slave of the zoo proprietor. In short, the pathological violence that breaks loose in zoo monkey "collections" is not simply the result of the unnatural stresses of zoo conditions, nor is it driven by an innate appetite for the violence and attraction of the behavioral sink. In its most real, political, and moral context it is the result of an act of violence by superstatus people who put baboons in zoos and transform them into commodities for human consumption. A true analogy is found in the stress conditions imposed on the people of Harlem by the dominant whites or by the zoo conditions imposed on the decultured Bantu by apartheid. The Bantu have also been converted into commodities for the cultural edification of white tourists, who are taken on conducted tours through the Bantu concentration camps.

The significant and unique factor in our human technological environment, for which there is no parallel in the monkey group, is the social isolation of people in overpopulated cities, which allows no scope for a direct and personal involvement with a living culture. This dialectic of "crowded isolation" and cultural alienation gives rise to both a pathological violence and a degenerate apathy. A valid analogy for this human dilemma cannot be found anywhere in wild primate societies, not even where diminishing space and population density has led to the violence of intraspecific killing. When establishment behaviorism warns us that we must pay full attention to the significance of space, the "territorial imperative," and the "human zoo" analogy, we are being told what we have known for a long time: that man like all primates is fundamentally a social animal dependent for his survival on a healthy group hierarchy, that he is innately aggressive, and that this natural aggression becomes pathological in conditions of extreme stress in the overpopulated cities. What we are not told is that the controllers of our competitive technological society have nurtured a corruption of the natural aggression drive of the human primate and that unless the dominant nations curb the destructive impulse for more power and more affluence, we shall destroy the biosphere of our planet. In physical terms we have an energy crisis. In moral terms we have a greed crisis. As Ivan Illich has said, contemporary society is ruled by "the ideology of unlimited progress."

Any comparative study on the function of aggression in primate societies is suspect when it is divorced from the politics of aggression. We must distinguish, therefore, between healthy and unhealthy aggression and recognize the distinct forms of phylogenetic aggression that characterize men of widely different cultures. For example, the Dani tribes in New Guinea engage in a ritualized form of war with other tribes. Few casualties occur in the course of several engagements over a whole year, and most of these are accidental. This highly ritualized form of ceremonial war is not motivated by a lust for ownership, dominance, and power. Its social significance is comparable with the competitive aggression that is released and ritualized in the Olympic games. The psychodynamics of these forms of culturalized aggression are not comparable with the militarized aggression of the Western nations. Nor is the latter comparable with the intraspecific violence that occurs in rat colonies under controlled and artificial conditions. A proper assessment of the different forms of aggression is unlikely to come from academic behaviorism, especially when a corrupted competitive aggression has become the motivating force of the very society it serves.

There are two distinct forms of establishment behaviorism, one overtly fascist and the other "liberal" or "humanistic." Where fascist behaviorism exploits the valid concept of an innate aggression, academic and reductionist behaviorism denies the spontaneity of phylogenetic aggression altogether. Aggression is explained either as a reaction to stress, or it is analyzed in terms of an abstract interaction between an animal and its ecology. All these vagaries will persist unless we stop thinking of aggression per se and come to terms with what I call the aggression-appeasement syndrome.

In order to live, reproduce, and stabilize the social code, all primate societies must draw upon their instinctual power to both aggress and appease. The lagothrix leader-monkey Jojo in our colony prefers peace, but he is ready to act aggressively to protect the group or to enforce the necessary disciplines within the group for maintaining peace and order. A submissive or appeasement gesture by a subadult during a dispute is nearly always accepted by Jojo as a sign of submission. Even quarrels among the subadult males are usually resolved by appeasement and not by aggression. The aggression drive is clearly all one with the inhibitory impulse to appease.

All the higher primates—men and monkeys alike—have one outstanding characteristic in common: both are susceptible to outbursts of passion and excitement, often from causes that seem trivial, yet they can be extremely sociable and affectionate. In no other animal species is the combination of violence and tenderness so intensely expressed. This is confirmed in the physiological fact that in monkeys (though much less than in man) there is a highly developed cortical control over a very powerful aggression drive. It follows that the survival of a stronger impulse to aggress depends equally on stronger inhibitory controls; otherwise the species would destroy itself.

Examples of this dramatic behavior are often seen in the woolly monkey colony, and the following is typical: The infant Ben has ventured some distance away from his mother Sadie and has been approached by a young female, Emma, who is only too happy to act as a substitute mother. Ben responds readily by *tuffing* and is about to climb onto Emma's back when up comes the young male Danny, who also wishes to be paternal and to fraternize with Ben. In the confusion Ben makes a number of high-pitched squeals expressing apprehension rather than fear. This draws the attention of the mother Sadie, who comes running over to investigate. Tension mounts when Ben finds himself surrounded by three overattentive monkeys, and he squeaks louder. Emma, with the best of intentions, persists in trying to console him. Danny, in the role of peacemaker, tries to appease Sadie, who is cough-barking (a high-pitched aggression sound) at Emma as though she were the cause of Ben's distress. The whole situation is the result of a most unfortunate misunderstanding, but it must somehow be resolved, otherwise it could lead to a serious fight between Sadie and Emma. This, however, could be averted by the intervention of the male, who may succeed in appeasing Sadie, provided Ben is reassured and back with her.

In such a conflict situation one often sees highly emotional and aggressive displays of threat and intimidation, accompanied by a crescendo of squeaks, cough-barks, and even screams of rage. In almost all cases, however, it is the inhibitory controls that take over, and just as suddenly as the incident began so it ends, with all parties in the dispute snuffling, sobbing, and huddling up to each other as though they wouldn't dream of treading on each other's toes.

Sexual disputes between males are rare. A subordinate male is unlikely even to approach a dominant male who is copulating. This in itself would be regarded as an act of aggression. However, in a critical situation involving two subdominant males of equal rank, one can never be sure how the conflict will be resolved. As the intruder approaches, the mating male may turn to face him and make the emotive cries and gestures of appeasement. His whole manner in sound and posture will seem to say: "I don't want to fight you—please don't interfere." This usually evokes a similar response in the intruder, who may move away. Should he, however, come closer still, the distinct displays in each monkey of threat and placation seem to interlock as tension mounts and fighting seems inevitable. Both monkeys, in fact, are expressing a psychological dilemma that transcends ritual and autonomous controls. So even at this stage the impulse to fight can be inhibited, not simply and directly by an autonomous control, but also by the disposition of the individual monkey to allow that control to operate.

We see then that the decision to fight or to appease in the monkey community will be determined to a large extent by the character and disposition of individual monkeys regardless of their rank. The highly emotional and temperamental behavior I have described is characteristic of the higher primates. Aggression (and appeasement) is found in many animal species, but in monkeys it is tempered by a degree of individual self-control. This endows the monkey with some freedom from the autonomy of fixed action patterns. Put simply, a monkey is able to decide whether it will or will not act in a certain way. That is why monkeys can be torn between decision and indecision, between the impulse to attack and the impulse to appease.

When aggression and appeasement are abstracted and posed as hawk and dove we see the fallacy of taking the dove as the harbinger of peace and the hawk as a predatory aggressor, since the hawk can just as easily be taken as a symbol of enterprise and health and the dove as a symbol of apathy. Clearly the functional dynamics of aggression and appeasement form a dialectic polarity; they presuppose each other. Appeasement acts positively for peace, and if peace degenerates, aggression acts positively with the object of restoring health. The polarity can be examined in the context of sickness or health, but to split the syndrome in two and treat one side only as the destructive element in relation to the other is to pose a false dichotomy that cannot be resolved in thought or reality. When either side gains a malignant ascendancy over the other, the syndrome as such is no longer a healthy representative of the aggression-appeasement impulse, but a pathological imbalance of its internal dynamics. Such an imbalance or disorder affects aggression and appeasement alike. In their place we have the double evil of a destructive aggression and a degenerate apathy, a pathological syndrome that is clearly at work in the dehumanizing of our consumer society. In its most severe form it is represented by the paranoid schizophrenic who is also subject to fits of manic depression.

It follows that aggression per se is neither sick nor destructive; it is simply the use of physical force to achieve a given end. Bad and good men are equally endowed with aggression. They are distinguished not by their use of aggression, but by how and why they aggress, by the values and motivations behind their specific acts of aggression. To say, therefore, that man by nature is innately aggressive can be a dangerous and misleading half-truth when it is abstracted from the other side of the coin, i.e., man is also by nature innately gentle.

Regardless of the distortions and vagaries from establishment science, the limitations of the ethological concept of aggression for comparative study remain clear to see. No true parallel exists in wild primate groups that corresponds with the positive action of liberation groups in human society. When evolution was faced by a similar problem (in a process called paedomorphosis), a whole species became extinct and a new beginning was made! But once we span the bridge from the instinctual dialectic of evolution to the conscious dialectic of history, we find that it is precisely the historical consciousness and historical action of enlightened minorities and individuals that is called upon to speak out, protest, and aggress against the system of a dead morality and create a new one.

I have considered the case for innate healthy aggression, but I have yet to explain the origin and function of an antisocial or "immoral" aggression that, in my view, is also innate and not simply a reaction to stress. This fundamental dilemma of the human psyche at war with itself has been man's concern since time began, and it would be a brave or a foolish man who believed himself to be without shame, at all times invulnerable to temptation and sin. The critics may claim that the problem must remain as such, as an enigma that is impervious to the concepts of history, science, and philosophy—even to art—and that it is better left to the mystics who have a taste for it. I do not agree. If my concept of a biological premorality is valid, it follows that a precursor of that behavior we sometimes call pathological and sometimes antisocial may also be at work in nature. My object in the next chapter will be to try to show that such an element of "biological immorality" is indeed foreshadowed in the psychology of our closest zoological relatives, the anthropoid apes, and that this immorality by its very nature is not necessarily pathological, nor does it have to be expressed in physical violence.

CHAPTER 5

The Birth of Sin

If there is a precursor to immorality in nature, we would not expect to find it in the growth of a crystal or the behavior of the fruit fly. Such a biological immorality must presuppose the functioning of the aggression-appeasement syndrome I considered in the previous chapter. Without this, those forms of behavior we sometimes call antisocial and sometimes criminal could not arise. Intraspecific aggression itself would not give us a prehistorical precursor to immorality because the essential quality of immorality is not aggression. Certainly the destructive effects of immoral action are that much greater when carried out with more aggression, but "more aggression" in itself, as we saw earlier, is not a step in the direction of immoral or pathological behavior.

There is a social form of intraspecific fighting and group hatred among rat clans that may be compared with immorality, but there is no psychogenetic impulse in the behavior of individual rats comparable with the premeditated, inquisitive, self-seeking, and cunning behavior of monkeys and apes. There is also a form of antisocial or "immoral" behavior peculiar to the higher primates that I call pathogenic. To explain its origin and function in primate evolution I must first dwell at some length on the unique and highly individualized character of monkeys and apes in which I believe this pathogenic element is rooted.

Fixed action patterns and highly ritualized behavior is less characteristic of wild primates compared with other animals. Much of the monkey's expressive behavior is so subtle and flexible that formal classification breaks down. There is, for example, a head gesture loosely called "cut-off," which refers to a quick sideways turn of the head. This gesture is usually interpreted by observers as a sign, meaning "I do not wish to be involved," made by one monkey to another. The term, however, hardly does justice to a wide range of motivational behavior that is expressed in different forms of this particular head gesture. To really understand these we must focus our attention on real incidents and real situations and less on formalized ritual. The following examples are typical:

1. An adolescent male is involved in a dominance dispute with an adult female. The leader Jojo intervenes on the side of the young male. The female screams her defiance, but Jojo turns his back on her and does *cut-off* with his chin lifted. This is a qualified cut-off, meaning "I don't wish to carry this any further, but you must do as I say."
2. Juvenile Polly approaches the dominant male Jimmy in one of the corridors and wishes to pass him without complications. Jimmy has not the least desire to prevent her from passing, and to reassure her he turns his head slowly to one side as a gesture of courtesy.
3. Suki is sitting on the grass near me, waiting impatiently for me to let her share my cup of tea. When I look at her she screws up her face and turns her head quickly to one side to express intense disapproval. I have known Suki for many years, and (if it were translated into English) I know she is saying, "I refuse to wait any longer. I am tremendously angry. When you look at me I can't stand the sight of your face, even though I am desperately in need of your attention."

Another link with hominid psychology is found in the kinship behavior of infant monkeys born of the same mother. The juveniles Danny and Charlie, who were born of the dominant female Lulu in our colony, play together and groom each other more frequently than they do with other juveniles in the colony. Lulu still comes to Danny's aid when he is in conflict with another juvenile, even though, as I write, he is two years old and biologically independent.

It has also been made clear to me that wild primates have a stronger sense of time. Our monkeys show a much greater awareness of varying intervals of time than any dog I have known. When I leave my study after a day's work all the dogs greet me with the same degree of enthusiasm as when I return home after an absence of a week. The monkeys greet me once only in the morning and then, as in the human family, take me for granted for the rest of the day. But the tremendous reception one receives from the monkeys after a week's absence from home clearly shows that they have a greater awareness of time passed than any of the nonprimate animals. Our monkey Samba used to walk across the room to get a cloth and return with it to put out a lighted match that was burning on the floor. She also kept in mind the use of the cloth when she fetched it for covering a new and strange object that caused her some alarm. These acts, as we shall see later, do not affirm a sense of "time projection," but they do display a high intelligence in terms of premeditated behavior.

We know that the juvenile in the monkey colony must try to exceed the limits of self-assertiveness in order to learn that it is unprofitable in the long run; thus he learns the right way and is happier for it. We also know that his social behavior and knowledge is not merely learned; it is innate. Thus far his behavior is similar to that of juveniles in most mammalian species. But one important distinction does emerge: the self-will of the individual monkey or ape operates on a new level of adaptive and creative ability, a level on which the innate potential for antisocial behavior is far greater. By virtue of this, even adult monkeys and apes can be antisocial in a most humanlike way. Typical is the antisocial cunning displayed by many of the Koshima Island monkeys, who waited until Imoko and her followers had washed the sweet potatoes and then intimidated and drove them away in order to profit by their labor. It is true that jackals will wait for the remains of the lions' prey, but no jackal or dog is capable of the "creative cunning" that is characteristic of the ape. Carole Gale, who worked with Jane Goodall's team on the Gombe Stream chimpanzee reserve in Tanzania, witnessed a most remarkable demonstration of chimpanzee cunning that is clearly comparable with the premeditated antisocial behavior of humans:

A group of females, mothers and infants were spending a quiet morning around a termite mound, digging for termites. Only one mother had managed to find a rewarding termite hole full of termites, and the rest were scratching around looking for the termites' tunnel openings but having little luck. Goblin, a juvenile of three, found a termite hole which the older females had missed. He was just beginning to dig when Gigi, an adult female, spotted him, and more importantly, spotted the hole he had found. She cunningly reached out a hand and tickled Goblin. He chuckled, and rolled over towards Gigi, kicking and patting her in return. She then tickled him vigorously until he laughed and was so completely involved in the play that he forgot his hole. Then swiftly Gigi stopped playing, reached over Goblin, and stole his termite hole![1]

Next to man no animal is more gifted or more cursed with the curiosity drive than the monkey or the ape. The monkey must investigate; he must find out what is underneath, above, behind, and, most important of all, what is *inside*. In his natural habitat nuts and fruits must be opened, for the best parts are inside. The yolk lies inside the egg. Grubs are found inside holes and under the bark of trees, and they must be poked out. Large insects wear their bones on the outside and they must be pulled apart to be eaten. Dangerous insects must be rendered harmless from the inside. The monkey and the surgeon therefore have much in common; both are dedicated to the inside and neither is likely to be led astray by outside appearances.

The degree of curiosity, inventiveness, and cunning displayed by the monkey in comparison with the dog is evident when one observes the social techniques of both animals in a human situation, when they are left to occupy themselves during what, from their point of view, may be described as a dull evening at home. Our Alsatian Max, for example, may be lying on a couch in the lounge with his eyes fixed on me. He can go out into the woods; he can fight the wolfhound Tim; he can grunt, sigh, go to sleep and dream, or stay awake. He can look at me because he is fed up and would like me to tell him what he wants to do. He may lift his head suddenly and give a low rumbling growl because a small sound outside has displeased him. In these circumstances he indulges in the greatest pastime known to dogs, and like the lions on the African plains when their bellies are full, he does nothing. In a similar situation the highly individualistic and adaptive intelligence of the monkey is apparent. This is illustrated in the following domestic extract (in the present tense) taken from my notes on the domestic behavior of woolly monkeys in a human environment:

Samba has just paid us a visit in the kitchen. She is now sitting down, looking the picture of innocence, while she contemplates a cupboard in the far corner of the room. Her problem is how to approach the cupboard and get the sherry bottle out without being noticed. This requires great skill, perfect timing, and a profound knowledge of human behavior patterns. Arriving there, she opens the door carefully and is now faced by the difficult problem of removing the bottle and taking out the cork, which must be done carefully and silently. Since the hand-thumbs of the woolly monkey move in parallel motion with the other fingers, she uses the opposable thumbs of her feet for a secure grip of the bottle. She is not an alcoholic, and she wants only the merest nip. With the first taste she shakes her head violently and smacks her lips with uncertain relish, because the taste both pleases and displeases at the same time. One more nip and the bottle is placed carefully down on the floor. I now walk over to her and wag a threatening finger in front of her nose, telling her how naughty she has been. She shows her gleaming white teeth and expresses the characteristic lagothrix chuckle of good humor: *huh*, *huh*. Samba in fact refuses to be demoralized.[2]

The foregoing incident is comparable with the behavior of the human rogue who cannot be demoralized, a person who puts up no rational defense when caught red-handed at some trickery, and who is incapable it would seem of sustaining a guilty conscience. Such a person was my old grandmother who used to cheat at cards. At the end of grandfather's reproach, even sometimes halfway through it, grandmother would burst into laughter, and the higher he raised his voice in disapproval, the more she would laugh. With tears streaming down her face and her enormous bosom shaking with mirth, it became increasingly difficult for grandfather to maintain his dignity. His reproach simply crumbled away, and there was nothing else he could do but join in the fun. This was not taken in good part by other members of the family, especially by those who had lost their money. My grandmother's social technique was remarkably like Samba's device of "chuckling" with good humor when reproached by me for stealing the sherry.

Purposeful Behavior

In the attempt to fix a critical stage in the transition from hominoids to hominids, primatologists have classified various stages in the use of tools, such as tool using, tool preparation, and toolmaking. The psychologist K. R. L. Hall believes that tool using is a behavioral adaption that evolved in the context of threat displays to inhibit attack. Although a "degree of purpose" may be at work in tool using by chimpanzees for obtaining food, Hall reasons that this behavior nevertheless is primarily the result of a behavioral adaption that is motivated by frustration, fear, and intimidation.[3] A similar "frustration" could of course have been experienced by the first chimpanzee who failed to dig termites from a hole with his fingers and in despair grabbed a nearby twig. Whether the first stick was used for striking another primate or poking into a termites' nest seems to me a rather fruitless enquiry. Significant for me is that once we are faced with a nonhuman primate that is able to use sticks and twigs constructively, it is bound to use them whether for fighting or food gathering. The origin of the new behavior is in the ability to overcome obstacles or relieve frustration in a more effective way.

A "tool" as such may even be improvised for aberrant sexual behavior. This was made clear to me by our monkey Elizabeth, an ex-pet who has failed to integrate successfully in a colony life. Elizabeth is obviously frustrated, yet she is quite unable to respond to the sexual overtures of the males. I believe this explains a habit she has of frequently prodding herself all over with a small stick or twig that happens to be lying close by. Her behavior evokes no interest or curiosity by other members of the group. They resigned themselves long ago to the fact that there is something peculiar about Elizabeth.

Equally unenlightening is Hall's explanation that wild primate "tool using" is rooted in the "manipulatory endowment" of the ape, so that threat gestures involving the actions of grasping, picking up, dropping, and throwing are autonomous and inevitable. My monkey friend Jessy has the physiological machinery for scraping the strings of a guitar, but her operations on the instrument are not simply the result of a "manipulatory endowment" fortuitously exploited in the context of threat displays or "frustration." Nor does this beg the alternative conclusion that she has a built-in potential for playing flamenco music. She *investigates* the guitar because she has an innate curiosity and compulsion to break down the mystery of any new and strange object or sound. Her behavior, however, is not a mere reflex to an unknown object. In its own phylogenetic context the behavior is both purposeful and intelligent.

To attribute the kind of purposeful action we have considered to "manipulatory endowment" does little more than draw the student's attention to a simple law of life: that one cannot scratch certain areas of one's back without A, the "manipulative endowment" for back scratching; B, a "conflict situation" that requires a "behavioral adaption" to an itch; and C, a back-scratching object (such as the branch of a tree or an umbrella) that happens to be lying around in the bathroom. The sum total of the back-scratching phenomenon is best understood, presumably, by studying the complex relationship between a back-itch frustration and the emergence of a suitable object for removing it, with no regard for the initiative displayed by the primate who is itchy.

The object of such analysis is clear: the explanation of behavioral adaption in a conflict situation is pushed to absurd limits in order to pose the old theory of adaption by circumstance as opposed to purposeful behavior, e.g., if the bath tap is too high to relieve the itch one makes a pathogenic grab for the umbrella. As C. R. Carpenter so rightly says: "When an adult spider monkey spans a space, remains suspended, and permits a young animal to cross it, is this too a 'primitive instrumental act?'"[4] It would seem that Hall's analytical method is to treat the tool-using behavior of primates as a sort of onion from which one coat is peeled off after another in order to find the real onion.

A distinction must be made between the spontaneous initiative displayed by a chimpanzee in discovering the use of an object and the use of a tool object by an animal species that required a vast period of time for the tool-using behavior to become fixed in compulsive autonomous action, such as the dam building of the beaver. Comparative study of the motivational behavior of different species will always break down when the motor impulses of fixed action patterns (such as the web spinning of the spider) are confused with the spontaneous potential in higher mammals for initiating new behavior and developing new skills in new situations. Tool using by monkeys and apes is not comparable with the phylogenetic feeding impulse of the woodpecker finch that uses a twig as an extension of its bill.

The fact that apes show a greater talent for recognizing and learning the use of tools in captivity is also highly significant. It demonstrates very clearly that they have a greater potential for understanding and mastering a variety of human skills than any of the nonprimate animals. To object that they do not display this potential to the same extent in the wild is to overlook that apes do not go careering around in the jungles riding bicycles, standing on boxes, blowing saxophones, and using the pot, though the juveniles, as is well known, do play "follow my leader." Their tool-using potential is confirmed in the fact that wild primate societies are the only societies that contain elements of culture and social behavior which point to the hominid lines.

Summing up, it is clear that all attempts to explain the origin of tool using in threat gestures, food gathering, or manipulative endowment inevitably fail to disclose the unique intelligence and psychology of the higher primate. There is in fact a distinct form of highly aggressive behavior that is peculiar to the mind of the ape. I am referring to a form of intimidation display that has been observed by Kortlandt, myself, and others, which is usually defined as the releasing of social tension. I believe this behavior requires definition in a wider context, which we are now ready to consider in some detail.

Unlike nonprimate mammals, apes are physiologically and phylogenetically programmed for swaying, stamping, beating, drumming, thumping, and throwing in the context of what I call pathogenic behavior. I regard this pathogenic element as an integral part of a unique intraspecific aggression that is peculiar only to monkeys, apes, and man. Apes cannot chant and dance in mimetic ritual like tribal man, but when they are stirred by the pelting rain and frightened by lightning and the crash of thunder, they will scream with rage, slap the ground, and stamp about in a frenzy of excitement. In their elementary way they are striving for the consummation of an act that will protect them from the forces of nature. Such instinctual and passionate action is the only defense they have against the invasion of a force that both terrifies and excites them. This they do while the other creatures of nature, whether lion or mouse, wait patiently and silently in cover or hiding until the fury of the storm has passed. Nonprimate animals are insensitive to the special kind of "fear" that invades and stimulates the psyche of the higher primates. I believe this pathogenic element is the most significant link between the psychology of man and that of the ape. Any field observer of chimpanzees in the wild will confirm the behavior I have described. When the storm rages along the South Cornish coast and invades the territory of our monkey colony, the dominant males Jojo, Jimmy, and Ricky will slash the ropes, throw objects about, and scream their defiance at the "unseen" invader. Here I believe is the key to the psychodynamics of the wild primate mind, but only in the context of its own environment and the given elements of a tool-using preculture.

In my view the evolution of the "tool" is best represented

by the following stages: tool using, tool preparation, tool carrying, tool retention, toolmaking, and "the making and keeping of a permanent cultural tool," each successive stage (or concept) to include the former. I would place chimpanzee tool using between the levels of tool carrying and tool retention, with Goodall's observation in mind of the Gombe Stream chimpanzee that carried a prepared stalk for half a mile to dig for termites in another hill. This retention may have been elicited by the immediate preoccupation with termite eating and not keeping for possible use in the future. In order to approach the levels of toolmaking and tool retention one must assume that the primate would have some vague awareness of abstract time or of time projection. Both preparing and retention could be an extension of "space and time" motivated by the immediate preoccupation and search for food.

I believe that tool preparation and carrying by the ape is undoubtedly purposeful action, but it does not in itself affirm a knowledge that transcends time. The legitimate tool as a cultural object did not emerge until the later hominoids or early hominids reached an elementary culture in which tool preparation and retention became a complete tool making and keeping for indefinite use in the future as well as the "now." As such, the thing we call a tool is a defined and permanent object that has no meaning outside the culture and the psychology of the primate who makes and owns it for the future as well as for the present. This presupposes the development of a language that includes a word for tool and a concept for time. We must now penetrate a little deeper into the origin of this "concept" in order to understand its importance for the theme of the present chapter.

The New Brain

It is evident when we take a first look at the nonprimate mammals that the sense of smell is one of the oldest. We see at once that the shape of the face is determined largely by the snout. But for tree-dwelling primates, who required binocular vision for rapid movement in the trees, the nose became relatively less important, and the development of binocular eyes essential for the manipulation of objects held in the hands. By working more with the hands and less with the mouth, the face was released from much of the physical work of finding food. The change, therefore, from muzzle to face made way for the frontal lobes of the brain to develop, which gave rise to a more complex system of sensory perception. Changes in the structure of the mouth and the larynx made possible a greater variety and range of vocal sounds, enabling the new primate to rely less upon ritualized behavior and more on communication by sound language and facial expression.

Once the forest primates had taken the first steps in a human direction, this direction was pursued by the man apes who followed. It was a period in which species of higher primates competed with nature and each other and became extinct, a period in which the elements of culture and tradition were taking root. A vast number of biological, social, and ecological changes acted together in the evolution of the new hominid lines: changes in climate, diet, and habitat; the discovery of fire and the making of tools; the development of erect body postures and of the hand and the organs of speech.

It is generally considered that the hominids became hunters when they were driven by hunger to leave the forests and hunt the herbivorous animals for food. On the plains and the grasslands they acquired a more erect posture and developed the longer legs of the runner instead of the long arms of the tree-dweller. Since the fastest runners are those with the thinnest hair coat, the hunting primates became relatively hairless compared with the forest dwellers; but by adopting the hunter's clothes of animal skins, they were able to spread beyond the temperate zones and survive the glacial periods. Planning for the hunt also required a new social organization and a system of communication more precise and articulate than the sounds and gestures of the forest primates. It is true that the early primates had evolved unique systems for signaling and vocal communication, but a language of imagery and concept was essential for expressing new objects and new relationships with more precision.

The new primate, *Homo sapiens*, was more resourceful in every way than his predecessors. He wore sewn clothes, made a variety of tools that he decorated with great skill, buried his dead with ceremony, and prepared them for an afterlife. A belief in a supernatural world could hardly arise among the frugivorous forest primates, for it was the dependence of the hunter on animals for food that gave rise to totemism and the worship of the animal spirits. Paleolithic man imitated his prey not only in sound and mime, but by donning the pelts of the animals he hunted, a habit that led to the wearing of animal masks in his magic ritual.

In his symbols and rites the Paleolithic savage identified his fear and aspirations with the natural forces that controlled his life. These powers were *conceived* as supernatural because their sources were unseen and unheard and, to that extent, unpredictable, inexplicable, and unknown. By collectively discharging his emotions in magico-ritual, the savage identified with the sacred spirits of the supramundane world and gave them a reality and an objective form. When he did this he was being logical, not alogical or prelogical. It was the beginning of the human process of transforming the unknown into the known. By ritualizing and objectifying his emotions and his needs in hunting magic, fertility dances, and totemic symbols, man also established a kinship between himself and the animal life on which he depended for survival. But this divine and terrifying situation, tense and fraught with danger, created a psychological dilemma, an emotional conflict and sense of guilt in the need to both worship and kill for food the very animals whose spirits (in their universality) controlled his life.

The spirits were logical constructions of an unseen universal that *had* to be given an objective reality, and in this context religion is a primitive form of our own philosophical concepts, which reconcile our history with the universal. The psychological conflict between kinship and killing was therefore discharged and objectified in ritual, art, and custom.

The social and spiritual significance of this divided mind, of a break from the biological animal to a pathogenic primate, is expressed in the face-painting art of the Caduveo Indians (see plates 11 and 12).

In native thought it is the design which confers upon the face its social existence, its human dignity, its spiritual significance. Split representation of the face, considered as a graphic device, thus expresses a deeper and more fundamental splitting, namely between the biological individual and the social person whom he must embody.[5]

A sublime form of the same conflict survives in a token custom practiced by the Amaha Indians, who leave a gift at the site of the plants they have gathered for medicines as a mark of respect for the soul of the plant. The question of whether these "nonliterate" Indians are less human and civilized than ourselves is aptly answered in the distinction they make between themselves and the whites: "Indians do not pick flowers."[6] Those of us who think our learning is superior and scoff at a people who refrain from gathering plants wantonly would do well to remember that a plant for the savage mind is a living thing in the larger scheme of nature. In his own spiritual way the savage finds in the animals and the plants those attributes with which he himself is endowed.

In my view the emotive impulse to eat and to love, to reconcile cruelty with kinship, is rooted in the conflict between violating and loving the spiritual force that controls all life. A precursor of this syndrome has been observed in the behavior of wild primates. On one occasion Carole Gale observed a dramatic display of the contradictory elements of appeasement and aggression in the behavior of an adult chimpanzee who had just captured a juvenile baboon. The chimpanzee was seen hugging the baboon close to his own body, in the same manner as the adult chimpanzee hugs an infant. At the same time his face was opened wide in the characteristic grimace of fear. This strange behavior was baffling for the observer until it was realized that the baboon was still alive. Only when it squirmed or screamed did the chimpanzee express fear and hug the baboon against himself. Between times he gnawed on the baboon's head and arm. When the head eventually hung limp and the animal showed little sign of life, the fear-hugging display ceased.

The behavior of chimpanzees during a tropical rainstorm is also a dramatic expression of both fear and excitement. Many humans have a primitive fear of thunder and lightning. Bocherd tells us that the dance ceremonies of the African bushmen during a thunderstorm are accompanied by wild cries, leaps, and drum beating on the *rommelpot*.[7] For the ape, who relies upon his alertness and keen senses to survive, this fear is stark and real: rain neutralizes the scent of the enemy, thunder consumes all other sounds of approaching danger, and lightning exposes the paths of retreat in the trees. In such an intense conflict situation the pathogenic action taken by the ape is the only defense he has against the forces of the unseen and the unknown. In this context, and that of the chimpanzee that both hugged and devoured its prey, in no other species with the exception of man is the combination of aggression and appeasement, of cruelty and tenderness, so intensely expressed. In human terms of the hate that fears and the love that conquers, I believe it is the fundamental drive of all creative behavior.

The ape is aware of what he sees and he knows well where to find food. He is alert to the dangers of the forest and skilled in avoiding them. He knows that the leopard and the snake are dangerous and he avoids them. He is aware of disease and knows that it brings pain. He is distressed and frightened by the tropical storms and by strange sounds that come from objects and places he cannot see. At the same time, he does not know why the food he gathers must grow or why it is sometimes scarce, or why the snake is poisonous, the night cold, or why the sun brings warmth. Similarly, the mother baboon will carry her dead baby around with her until it decomposes in her arms. She is distressed and aware of the fact that the baby does not behave as though it were alive, but she does not know that it is dead.

Whereas the man apes took their existence for granted, the

human primate came face to face with himself and therefore
with his future and his past. With this new sense of time came
the challenge and the fear of death and the need to invoke the
spirits of good and evil to allay that fear and ensure immortality, particularly when the fear was stimulated by the conflict
between killing and worshiping the animal spirits who controlled his life. The concept therefore came with man's discovery of the unknown and the supernatural, a concept that
united the unknown with the known and that grew out of
man's struggle with the forces of life and death. In an ethno-
musicological context, the new level of evolutionary consciousness was also a new sense of rhythmic unity, of the
rhythm made by man, which is the root of all his chant and
dance ritual. This rhythmic power, like the concept in relation
to the "things named," subordinated all other specific sounds
in nature (whether arhythmic or rhythmic) to it. The point is
taken up by the musicologist Dr. Marius Schneider: "Man is
distinguished by his polyrhythmic constitution. He is not only
able to produce the sound peculiar to his own nature, but also
to imitate non-human rhythms and sound colours. Anyone
who knows and can imitate the specific sound of an object is
also in possession of the energy with which the object is
charged."[8]

Although an idea expressed in music is less articulate than
when it is expressed in words, the musical expression gives the
idea an emotional force, a mysterious objectivity that transcends the spoken word. When the aborigine sings the name of
the totem god he brings the spirit into his own voice and
forces him to be present, just as one can produce a sympathetic vibration on an open string by sounding the same note
on another string. The aborigine regards the objects of nature
as the dwelling places of the spirits and the sounds of the
natural world—the flapping of wings and the groaning of trees
—as the voices of the spirits. In Australian mythology these
spirits were the ancestors of man. They created everything in
nature and taught men the rituals that were necessary for preserving life. When the aborigine dances the movements of the

kangaroo, he identifies himself with his totem god and he really believes that he is a kangaroo.

A striking example of the creative energy that is released in the rhythmic power of dance is found in the molimo fire dance of the Ituri pygmies. This ritual, performed at times of great crisis, is accompanied by the voice of the molimo trumpet, an instrument that reproduces all the sounds of the forest —the buffalo and the leopard, the call of the elephant, and the plaintive cooing of the dove. At the climax of the fire dance a circle of men dance around an old woman who, in a burst of frenzied shouting, rushes into the flames and scatters the glowing embers in all directions. The men dance in a wild circle, and as they dance their bodies sway backward and forward, facing the fire, as though by imitation of the act of generation they are giving the fire new life. It is said that this ritualized dance has its origin in an ancient legend that tells of a time when the women owned the sacred molimo, a time when "a woman stole the fire from the chimpanzees."[9]

In an earlier chapter I considered how group survival among the nonprimate animals requires the observance of social codes that are genetically programmed and expressed almost entirely in fixed action patterns. In man, and also to a significant degree among monkeys and apes, there is a new and stronger element of freedom from the domination of autonomous instinctual impulses. This heightened consciousness of the ability to inhibit self-assertiveness still works for the same ends—survival, health, and stability—but unlike the autonomous controls it is also self-inhibitory. In short, it becomes an animal that is both cursed and blessed with a conscience. This conscience is confirmed in the physiological fact that the highly specialized cortical control of aggression and sexual behavior in man distinguishes him from other animals. The survival value of stronger aggressive-sexual drives depends equally on stronger inhibitory controls, and it is this unique intraspecific aggression discussed earlier of monkeys and apes that is historically continuous with the pathogenic conscience of man. Such a pathogenic inheritance brings in its wake a heightened awareness of fear, shame, separateness, sociability, courage, loyalty, and love. This conscience, however, is not (as so many ethologists and psychologists seem to think) in opposition to the instinctual machinery of autonomous controls; it is continuous with them, though it must inevitably experience conflict between the dogma of nature and its newly found freedom in order to be a decision maker and to know itself as an individual. The consciousness of "I am" therefore spans the evolutionary bridge from the perception of the object as a "thing in itself" to a conception of its meaning for the observer.

The conceptual power of the new primate brain was no less compulsive than the instinctual mind of the earlier primates. The "split" between reason and instinct that we hear so much about was not an evolutionary mistake in brain building; it was a primate breakthrough that provided man with a new tool and a new source of energy. It was also a new challenge to survival, and with its blessings came new threats, new dangers, and entirely new techniques for both creation and destruction.

The ape-men who left the forests to hunt on the plains became more separated from the family group. Their new way of life strengthened comradeship, but it also stimulated an appetite for personal ownership. When they went hunting and left their women and children at a fixed home base they were able to exploit the new division of labor within the social group to their own advantage. They had inherited the stronger physique and innate dominance behavior from the forest primates, and the role of predator no doubt helped to boost the primate ego. With their new pattern of life also came the ownership of the tools and weapons for hunting and control of the kill before returning to the home base. Hunting techniques, tracking, and organization strengthened male cooperation and a sense of comradeship, just as the Amazon hunters today will communicate across the rivers in a special sound language with the flute. Children also took longer to reach biological maturity than the children of the forest primates, and the freedom of the hunter was increased by the need to leave the responsibilities of child care almost entirely to women. These factors also played their part in inviting and developing an appetite for ownership and power, and one could say it was inevitable that the first men would exploit "temptation," whether provided by Satan in the Garden of Eden or by natural selection in a patriarchal habitat.

Individuality in the ape is not phylogenetically programmed for imposing the antisocial will in a way that constitutes a threat to the survival of the group. In man, where the psychodynamics of the emotive will operate on a higher level of individuality, the psychological conflict between kinship and killing presupposes an awareness of the power to will and to act for self only, and more significantly, the political power to conspire with others for organized oppression. The inevitable result of such a potential was war on other tribes and the economic exploitation of slaves, women, and children. In these conditions natural rites became institutionalized into dogma, and patriarchal hierarchies evolved with an authority as oppressive as any found in the secret societies of tribal peoples in precolonial Africa and North America.

The Fall of Man is only a myth, but it is a very real one. The pathogenic impulse for love and hate brought a new loyalty and a new sense of responsibility into the mind and the life of the savage and with it a power of envy that inspired him to exploit and dominate his brother. But without the action of slavery and greed the human race could never have discovered its own humanity. Without sin there could never have been shame, and without shame no way of transcending our private obsessions. I think we must therefore see the Fall of Man as the Rise of Man, since our history has been made by good men as well as bad. That, at any rate, will be my starting point for taking a closer look at the face of evil in a later chapter. But first I must prepare the ground by examining another area of primate evolution, of what has been called "the hominization process."

CHAPTER 6

From Hominoid to Hominid

The little we know about the life of extinct species of subhuman primates is based on the anatomical remains discovered by paleontologists. Existing fossil collections of the later subhuman primates (hominoids) now contain a number of new finds of complete skulls, near-complete skeletons, and bones of limbs, hands, and feet. Analysis shows that these Upper Miocene hominoids lived from 10 to 16 million years ago.

There are a number of nominees as "links" between the hominoid lines (anthropoid apes and many related species now extinct) and the hominids (*Australopithecenes*, *Pithecanthropus*, Neanderthaler, and *Homo sapiens*). Famous among these is *Oriopithecus*, an arboreal primate with an almost equal share of the anatomical and behavioral characters of both the hominoids and the early hominids. Another species with hominid characters similar to *Oriopithecus* is *Ramapithecus*, which Leakey has assigned to the species *Kenyapithecus*. The general conclusion is that these advanced hominoid species were living in both Africa and India from the late Miocene to the early Pliocene.

A near-complete skeleton of *Oriopithecus* was found by Hürzeler in 1958.[1] The creature weighed about ninety pounds, was about four feet high, and had a number of manlike features not found in the anthropoid apes: nasal spine and bone projecting beyond the level of the face; steep lower jaw; small and short canines; short lower arm bones; limb bones less efficient for brachiation. A gap in the palate between the canines and the lateral incisors, which is normal among apes but hardly ever occurs in living men, was found in only one of twelve *Oriopithecus* specimens.[2]

At the moment *Oriopithecus* is classed as a manlike "swamp ape" in the order of the hominoids (anthropoid apes), but many primate paleontologists are not satisfied with this classification. Whatever *Oriopithecus* was, ape-man or man ape, with new finds from new sites, particularly in China and South Africa, the problem is no longer one of establishing a "missing link," but of knowing where to place an increasing number and variety of primate lines between the existing orders of the hominoids and hominids. Paleontologists have in fact already divided the hominids into *Homo erectus* and *Homo sapiens*.

For the present the hominids are distinguished from the hominoids by the behavioral characters of the former in the use of stone tools, a distinction that obviously is not going to hold fast for very long. Disregarding new finds, which in time must lead to the classification of new orders, the behavioral "line of demarcation" between the hominoids and hominids is already on shaky ground because of new evidence from the field of primate ethology. As we noted in the previous chapter, elements of a social tradition in toolmaking and in hunting have been observed in the behavior of chimpanzees and baboons in the wild.

Following the hominoids in the human direction are the *Australopithecenes*. Our knowledge of these early hominids has come from the work of such anatomists and paleontologists as Dart, Broom, Robinson, and Leakey. Dart discovered depressions on baboons' skulls as evidence that *Australopithecenes* hunted, and bones of predatory kills were found in a cave at Makapansgat. Pebble tools were also found on the site. A study of the postcranial skeleton showed that none of these early fossil men used the same sitting posture as modern man, nor did they walk as erect as we do. The position of the arm in relation to the shoulder is apelike, and the evidence suggests they put more muscular strain on their arms and hands.[3] In

1959 Leakey discovered a fossil manlike primate in the Olduvai Gorge, an *Australopithecene* since named *Zinjanthropus* and classified as a hominid. Crude stone "tools" and bones of eaten animals were found in the site. The tools were sharp enough for cutting skin that *Zinjanthropus* could not tear with his teeth or soften with fire. The bones suggest that he had just begun to hunt and that his quarry must have been slow-moving game, similar to that captured by wild chimpanzees and baboons.

The next most likely representative in the evolutionary direction of *Homo sapiens* is *Sinanthropus pekinensis*, commonly known as Peking man. He was discovered in the Lower Pleistocene strata near Choukoutien in China. Pebble and flake implements, which had been shaped with a hammerstone, were found in the caves. His method of chipping shows that he was right-handed, a human trait that is determined by the dominance of one side of the brain. A great variety of animal bones, such as bear, bison, hyena, and horse, were found with his own remains in the caves, and there is no doubt that he was a skilled hunter. He also used fire extensively.

In a Paleolithic culture known as the Mousterian, we find the closest *Homo* precursors of modern man, the Neander-thalers, who are hardly distinguishable from the early *Homo sapiens*. People with the physiological characteristics of Neanderthalers lived in caves and adapted to severe climates by wearing animal pelts. They made stone flake-tools, wood spears, heart-shaped hand axes, and flint-point spearheads. They hunted rhinoceros, mammoth, and bear, and they cut the carcasses and cooked their meat. At a Neanderthaler site in the Dordogne, polished tools of rock crystal were found, which clearly display an artistic sense. At Monte Circio a Neanderthaler skull was discovered within a circle of stones in a small inner chamber, and heaped around the walls were also the bones of hyena, horse, lion, and elephant.[4] Near Peyzac in the Dordogne, the skeleton of a Neanderthaler youth was discovered lying with the back upward and with the head and forearm resting on a pile of flint flakes. At the side was a hand

A Primate Family Tree

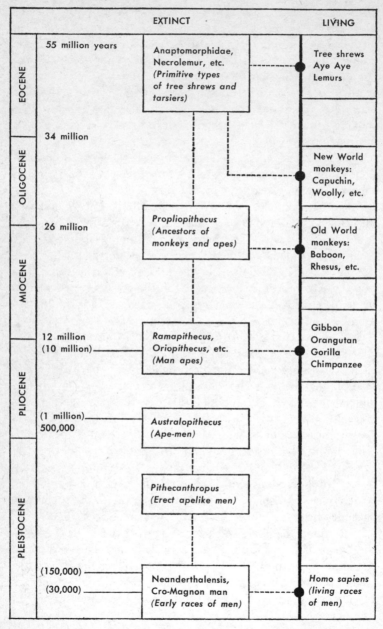

ax and the charred bones of an ox. It is considered by many that the contents of the grave were the remains of a funeral ceremony.[5]

The first undisputed representative of modern man is Cro-Magnon, who arrived in Western Europe during the late Paleolithic. Fossil skeletons and muscle insertions show that he was about five feet nine inches tall and powerfully built. His skull was long and large, the face broad across the cheekbones, and the forehead high with slightly thickened superorbital ridges. Many of his encampments have been discovered in the open as well as beneath overhanging rocks. Apart from a vast quantity of finds, which show clearly that he made bone articles for domestic use, such as needles and clasps and superbly fashioned knives, drills, and scrapers, his art and ritual is recorded for all to see in the well-known cave paintings at Les Trois, Catalonia, and La Mouthe.

The brief sketch I have given of the evolution of the primates from the early Pliocene to the Upper Paleolithic covers a time span of some 20 million years. The summary and chart that follow will I hope help to fix in mind a broad pattern of this process of hominization so that a more unified picture of man will emerge when we consider the sociocultural levels of hominid evolution. Because many species and their genera were contemporary or in close succession, their relation to the chronological periods and the time spans given are of course only rough approximations. A sample of the *Zinjanthropus* "level," for example, averages 1,750,000 years ago.[6]

(1) *Late Miocene to early Pleistocene* 10 to 16 million (years ago) Hominoids (man apes), *Oriopithecus, Ramapithecus, Kenyapithecus*

(2) *Lower Pleistocene* 1,500,000 to 500,000 Hominids (ape-men); *Australopithecus: Zinjanthropus, Paranthropus*

(3) *Middle Pleistocene* 500,000 to 150,000 *Homo erectus; Pithecanthropus*: Peking man, Java man

(4) *Upper Pleistocene* 150,000 to 30,000

Homo neanderthalensis, early precursors of *Homo sapiens*
(5) *Upper Paleolithic* 30,000 years
Homo sapiens (modern man), Cro-Magnon man

It is true that many species of hominoids and hominids were contemporaries with their own specific histories and cultures, but this does not invalidate the deduction that successive "races" of *Homo neanderthalensis,* for example, passed through sociocultural levels that were continuous as well as discontinuous with those of *Pithecanthropus.* Evolutionary concepts cannot be usefully constructed merely by the arrangement of fossil hominids into a morphological series abstracted from space and time. Useful synthesis must also consider the phylogeny of primates and the chronological significance of their sociocultural levels. Only in this way can evolutionary concepts that would otherwise remain static in prehistory be broken down and made continuous with history. As long as this is understood, we are now ready to consider some of the confusions and problems that have recently arisen in the failure to relate the dynamics of evolutionary change with the social structures and behavioral characters of specific cultures.

1 Leader male on his way back from the trees

2 Tower and tree platform linking outdoor houses to the trees

3 & 4 Outdoor play and social activity

5 & 6 Foraging in outdoor territory

7

The male Jimmy approaches
Jessy and waits for the infant
to show some interest in him.

8

The greeting here is actually
initiated by the infant.

9

The mother approves of this
social event and responds by
grooming the male.

10 Jojo, leader of the group

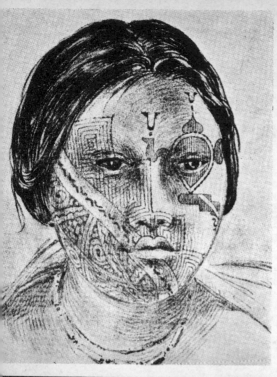

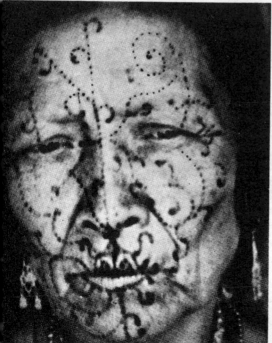

11 & 12

Split representation in the face painting of the Caduveo Indians (see page 55)

a.

b.

c.

13

Dani children (see page 141)
a. Building play houses
b. Children who no longer
   feed from their mothers
   often seek comfort at the
   breast.
c. A bow thong gives a small
   boy practice in making the
   sounds for a mouth harp.
d. Attending to domestic
   pigs

d.

14 The village game with Arancaria seeds

15 Spear-the-hoop game

CHAPTER 7

The Biocultural Miracle

We know that a series of genetic changes in the evolution of the primate lines gave rise to a number of tool-keeping, talking, and cultural animals known as the hominids and that only one of these species, *Homo sapiens*, has survived. With the subsequent growth of their accumulated culture, it has been tacitly assumed by most investigators in the biological sciences that their phylogeny or genetic evolution came to a standstill.

A growing body of evidence from the field of primate paleonotology has made an anatomical distinction between the subhuman and human primates increasingly arbitrary; a sharp division cannot be established. The evidence confirms that a biological "transition" as such from ape-man to man was one of degrees, but the question of whether or not the human psyche also evolved by degrees remains unanswered. Considered empirically, the inbuilt or genetic capacity for culture seems to have evolved gradually by degrees over a vast period of time. These degrees, however, are always considered quantitatively, not qualitatively. For a strange reason best known to many "evolutionists" and physical anthropologists, a qualitative mutation is always reserved for a genetic "leap" from the unfulfilled ape-man to "complete man." The American anthropologist Arthur Kroeber writes: "The development of the capacity for acquiring culture was a sudden, all-or-none quantum-leap type of occurrence in the phylogeny of primates."[1] It is clear that this astonishing confusion begins with the postulation of a single psychological prototype, in which the full complex of the human psyche is supposed to reside, a "human" prototype, presumably, with an inbuilt potential for speaking like Socrates, thinking like Kant, and creating like Leonardo da Vinci. We know that mutations and "genetic leaps" can be as sudden as the flare of a match, but they are not miracles by which an Australopithecene man ape jumps out of the subconscious of nature into the consciousness of history.

It is already apparent that a vast number of species of sub-men can be taken to represent a series of subconscious, precon-scious, and self-conscious levels, all of which must have been both genetically and culturally determined in "leaps" or "de-grees" that were distinct in quality as well as quantity. Unless we consider the evolution of the human psyche in this context, we shall always be faced with a choice between a genetic miracle or a smooth curve of imperceptible change. Neither the "miracle" nor the "unbroken path" will tell us anything about the dynamics of evolutionary change.

This theory of what I call the "biocultural miracle," by which "true" men and "true" culture are supposed to have burst upon the evolutionary scene in one jump, is still a fa-vorite piece among academics in socioanthropology and com-parative psychology. The sentiment is rooted in the concept of the "psychic unity of mankind," which refers to the fact that there are no fundamental differences in the cultural and con-ceptual abilities of the various races of man. Once a concession is made to significant differences among the early races of *Homo sapiens*, it is feared that the path is set for racial discrim-ination. So strong is this feeling (and understandably so) that many physical anthropologists are already pressing the concept of *Homo sapiens* to embrace all "races" of early Neanderthaler. Certainly Neanderthaler had a well-defined culture, and if culture is going to be equated with "humanity" in the context of the "biocultural miracle," it would follow that Neander-thalers must be accepted as true representatives of the human race. The same could of course be said of Peking man, who also had a rudimentary culture. Just how far this will go is difficult to guess. I personally have no objection to including chimpanzees in the order of *Homo sapiens,* provided the chimpanzees are agreeable.

Clearly the confusion is between races and species. If species emerged step by step, then so did cultures. I can see nò reason for assuming that the biological and psychogenetic capacity for culture was an all-or-nothing event and that once achieved all further history was built up on the basis of cultural expansion and the accumulation of new techniques and customs.

We know that Peking man (*Pithecanthropus*) had a rudimentary culture. He made simple tools, hunted large game (which required group cooperation), and he must have possessed a more precise and wider range of vocal and sign communication than any we find among the hominoid primates. Even though a smaller brain size does not necessarily mean an inferior intelligence, when the smaller brain of Peking man is considered together with other characters such as heavy brow ridges, sloping forehead, and large palate and teeth, it is clear that he represents a hominid species genetically and anatomically distinct from the Neanderthalers that followed him. It follows, as archaeological evidence has shown, that their cultures were also distinct as well as continuous. The question, therefore, as to whether biological mutations and cortical expansion preceded or followed the beginning of new cultures is meaningless. It is obvious that new skills and techniques were dependent on the development of brain growth, but this brain growth was equally dependent on the initiators (whether considered as individuals or species) of those skills. Of course, selection pressures must favor those individuals and species with greater skills as long as we remember (1) new skills are built up on customs and techniques already given and (2) the decision makers and the initiators of new customs, techniques, and skills must also exist and act before the selective pressures can select! Indeed, it is because man is phylogenetically programmed for the culture into which he is born that he is able to create as well as adapt to culture.

I have labored my point for the following reason: as long as the concept of "the psychic unity of man" imposes a genetic barrier between "species" and "races," it is forced to sandwich a "biocultural miracle" between prehistory and history (thus breaking their continuity) and at the same time to deny the possibility of any future phylogenetic change in the animal we call man. I shall return to this later. For the moment I want to show how the fallacy of the "biocultural miracle" is all one with the popular theory of an increasing "gap" between man's innate behavior impulses and his expanding culture.

It has been said that ". . . the symbolic network with which we live provides for us the mechanisms for ordered behaviour which in lower animals are genetically built-in to their bodies but which in ourselves are not."[2] Where is the evidence for assuming that man has no phylogenetic motivation for social behavior? Of course, there is a "gap" between the emotive machinery of phylogenetic behavior and what has to be socially learned and acquired, but that is not a unique character of the human primate.

When you have lived side by side as I have with a social group of wild monkeys and watched six infant monkeys born, grow, adapt, assert their individuality, and learn the social codes of the monkey group, you appreciate that they too have a great deal to learn. When we say that man is phylogenetically prepared in the womb for the culture into which he is born, we do not mean that he is born with a ready-made technique for playing the violin or with the moral prejudice for joining the Salvation Army. A man matures biologically and morally from child to adult because he is able to learn the disciplines of his culture, a culture on which he depends for the realization of his own independence, and this he achieves by conforming or dissenting, vegetating or creating, and even with the choice of living or dying for his principles.

Man's built-in capacity for creating as well as adapting to culture has developed by qualitative degrees over a long period of time, during which a vast body of institutionalized knowledge has accumulated that man in general must learn. This does not of course mean that the individual man must learn the sum total of his cultural heritage in order to integrate successfully in his society, any more than a monkey has to learn all the individual characters of the entire plant and animal life in its own habitat before it can climb and eat. Now if we wish to dramatize the power and the enormity of our cultural heritage in comparison with the emotive mechanisms the human animal is born with, it is very easy to paint a picture of "unqualified" and "untaught" man as a congenital idiot. But a monkey that is taken away from its mother, the disciplines of a group hierarchy, and a natural environment in the jungle, and then put in a cage to grow up as an unqualified isolate also becomes a pathological vegetable or a desocialized neurotic. In short, human culture and human phylogeny are integral, as is monkey society to monkey phylogeny: each demands and implies the other. We agree, as one writer has said, that " . . . a cultureless human being would probably turn out to be not an intrinsically talented though unfulfilled ape, but a wholly mindless and consequently unworkable monstrosity." But we agree only to the extent that the "cultureless human being" be taken as a hypothetical isolate, or a human being that is born on an uninhabited island and raised in a colony of ants, where in science fiction it may grow up to be a superant. It is not a question of whether human behavior is "more" dependent on cultural symbols and institutions compared with chimpanzees in relation to chimpanzee precultures; human behavior is as integrally dependent upon its own expanding culture as that culture is dependent upon it. To sum up: the relative "gap" between instinctual and learned knowledge is no greater for a human than it is for a chimpanzee. The theory of the "widening gap" is a false equation.

The built-in social conscience of human primates has been interpreted by one authority as a piece of "obsolete emotive physiology" that has become maladaptive for our present environment:

Since cultural change has moved much more rapidly than genetic change, the emotional response tendencies that have been built into us through their suitability for a long succession of past environments may be less suitable for the very different *present* environment. In this sense, there may be some respects in which modern man is obsolete.[3]

Here we are faced with another variation on the theme of the "widening gap" between man's instincts and his culture, in an extraordinary piece of speculation that takes the abstraction "present environment" as the criterion for health and survival. It overlooks the fact that the central element in the psychology of all hunters and gatherers in prehistoric and existing savage tribes is the kinship of mutual aid, by which the laws of a domestic economy are extended beyond local tribes: "Among all hunters and gatherers there is constant give and take of vital goods through hospitality and gift exchange. Everywhere generosity is a great social value . . . . Where kinship is extended beyond the local group, so are reciprocity and mutual aid."[4]

It is in fact the very alienation of the modern domestic family from a direct, personal, and responsible involvement with a living group culture, whether of small or large communities, that constitutes one of the most destructive features of life in our technological environment. In this context the "emotive physiology" of the human animal for a cultural identity (which has evolved over millions of years in the phylogeny of the hominids) is now in conflict with a dehumanized power structure that feeds on the anonymous consumer. The emotive physiology of this power structure may well be obsolete, but not the instinct for continuity that impels natural men to oppose it.

Once we have disposed of these spurious theories of "the cultural gap" and "obsolete emotive physiology," we are again in touch with history and the political nature of the tasks that confront us. It will also enable us to explode another myth in contemporary socioethological theory: that the main cause of war and mass killing is man's lack of an instinctual inhibition against "long-distance" killing. The theory is based on the proposition that no inhibiting motor impulse is evoked in the use of long-range weapons against a distant or an invisible enemy, compared, for example, with the raven's instinctual inhibition against directing its beak at the eyes of a brother. The implication is that if modern men had horns and tusks they would be less likely to kill one another. I would suggest that if the Detroit police (who lynched the black men in the *Algiers Motel Incident*) had horns and tusks they might gore to death every black man they ran into on sight. These new forms of social Darwinism would suggest that it is the apolitical ethologist who has no inbuilt instinct for assessing a destructive culture that condones long-range or short-range killing in the name of "national survival."

Even if the analogies I have considered were useful, we would still have to come to terms with the kind of "men" we are talking about. Long-distance killing, for example, may be uninhibiting for a pathological "democracy" that instructs brainwashed primates to bomb women and children, but such "action patterns" are anything but impersonal for those who are morally outraged by what is clearly an overt crime against humanity.

Where does the moral force of those who protest come from? Regardless of cultural conditioning, a psychological predisposition for its evolution must also be accounted for. We know that face-to-face inhibitory behavior is innate in human phylogeny, so why should we assume that the moral condemnation of nuclear war (and the refusal of dissenters to have anything to do with it) is only intellectually and culturally acquired? As I tried to show earlier, there is no reason to suppose that cultural development has grown independently of further organic development of the human psyche. Action taken by the ethical will for social ideals that transcend the political amorality of the militarized state may give rise to a psychogenetic change that is continuous with an inherited sense of instinctual morality.

It is generally considered that changes in the gene complex are rare events and that vast periods of time are required for the inheritance of structural adaptions (such as the squatting facets in the fetus of the Indian Punjabis) to become stabilized. Such early biological adaptions, however, were "rare" only in relation to the tempo of their own histories. What we must look for is not a major biological mutation in the context of prehistorical time, but a rapid and more subtle mutation in the human psyche that matches the explosive tempo of a nuclear society, a society unparalleled in history for its rapid accumulation of destructive power. Faced by such a devastating challenge, new and revolutionary insights may well become fixed in the instinctual machinery of a new morality, and for all we know, such mutations and genetic recombinations have already occurred.

Those who prefer to wait for the brain surgeon or the molecular chemist to heal the so-called paranoiac split between instinct and reason may well be alarmed by the new morality of revolutionary dissenters who are fighting for a natural culture, for a society that will be inhibited against murder, whether long-distance or otherwise. And they are doing this with or without the inheritance of "autonomous inhibitory impulses" and regardless of the dogma of rare and accidental mutations in the gene complex.

CHAPTER 8

The Smile of Hope

In a technological society that puts brains before the arts it is to be expected that the "analytical intelligence" of the individual will become the measure of his economic worth. In such a society the significance of the emotional maturity of the human animal is likely to be overlooked, and it is hardly surprising to find that this obsession with "mental ability" is also at work in comparative studies of animal behavior.

Among the most fruitless and wearisome of experiments in this field of investigation have been those concerned with measuring the relative development of the human child and the ape child. We know the formulas well: a baby chimpanzee is reared alongside a human baby. The baby chimpanzee "overtakes" the human baby in all fields during the first eighteen months or so. While the human infant at the age of nine months is sucking its thumb, the chimpanzee is unlocking a door or riding a bicycle. Then, lo and behold, the human infant learns a few words and begins to show a "superior intelligence" (as though it had not always done so from the moment of its birth!), and by the time it is eighteen months or two years old it begins to overtake the chimpanzee. Here the "comparative study" ends, with the conclusion that "intelligence" in the chimpanzee develops more rapidly than in the human infant during the first eighteen months or so of its life and that during this period the chimpanzee displays a greater ability for solving problems and learning new skills.

The official zoological explanation for the mental "superiority" of the chimpanzee during the first eighteen months is that the brain growth of the human is much slower compared with that of the chimpanzee. In man, puberty is reached at twelve to fourteen years, and brain growth is not completed until twenty-one to twenty-three years. The brain growth of a chimpanzee is completed in three years, and puberty is reached at about seven years. This change in the comparative growth rates of the brain in relation to puberty is the result of a change called neoteny, by which infantile traits in the fetus are retained and allowed to develop into adult life.

Because of its relevance for the present chapter, it is important to understand clearly the biological significance of this zoological concept of neoteny. In the fetus of an unborn mammal like the bear, for example, the head is at right angles to the trunk. Just before birth the head rotates in line with the trunk so that the animal can see ahead as well as directing the head for contact with the ground. In man, and to a lesser extent in apes and monkeys, the fetal angle of the mammalian head (which is at right angles to the trunk) is retained so that the head is facing forward. In this way the erect primate man can develop a brain that is able to exploit the advantages of free hands, longer thumbs, vertical walking, a longer neck, and a more direct frontal vision. It follows logically that more time is required for the built-in potential of such a brain to mature, a great deal more than is required for reaching biological maturity in terms of puberty.

This longer period of brain growth, compared with the growth rate of the reproductive organs, is always referred to by zoologists as a "slowing down" of mental growth in relation to the more rapid attainment of sexual development, resulting in sexual maturity being reached long before "mental maturity." Now this "mental maturity" is a vague concept. If it refers to a maximum efficiency of the "intelligence" (as would be measured in the so-called IQ tests) that coincides with the end of brain growth, then the point (with some reservations) may be taken. But if it means the maturity of the mind in terms of conceptual, moral, and intuitive development, then the answer must quite definitely be no, because no one yet has been able to define and assess the full potential of the human mind, least of all in biological terms.

Clearly the whole development of the human primate is extended both psychologically and organically, and more time is required for this to take place. It will also alter the relative growth rate of instinctual and intellectual maturity, of the reproductive organs in relation to the brain, of autonomous behavior and conscious behavior, if only because the development of a mature penis before the development of a mature psyche has already been favored by natural selection, and, in my experience and observations, by most men as well!

Whatever the psychodynamics of the infant psyche may be, we can be sure that it is not the "ape play-stage" that is retained in the development of the human psyche, but the beginning of a phylogenetically new and human creative stage. The failure to recognize this leads to the claim that "intelligence" in the chimpanzee develops more rapidly than in the human infant and that because of this the chimpanzee is able to strike a match, for example, long before the human infant is able to open the box. What can be said is that chimpanzee intelligence develops more quickly than human intelligence, which is so obvious that one begins to wonder what the object was in making such a comparative study in the first place. Nothing is gained unless we disclose the nature and the function of what is unique about the psyche of the human infant. In reality, as we shall see later, the chimpanzee infant is already "behind" the human infant at the moment of birth and even before birth. A new technique of holography in brain research has in fact confirmed the phylogenetic inheritance of a language capacity in the human infant. In a paper to the 1968 conference of the Royal Society, J. P. Thorn said,

It is becoming evident that we are actually born knowing the deep structure of language. Without this inborn "grammar" a small child would never be able to learn the infinite variety of speech sounds it encounters. . . . Memory studies must therefore take account of inborn knowledge of language, the learning of a particular language, and the extraordinary capacity to relate these to the rapid streams of speech sounds we hear.

This brings us back to the starting point of my case: by concentrating exclusively on a comparison of "mental development" in two species, chimpanzees and *Homo sapiens*, two distinct psychological and motivational levels of behavior are confused and compounded as one. A proper understanding of these distinct psychogenetic levels is not possible until each is examined and compared in its own context, i.e., with full regard for the total complex of psychological phenomena (not merely an abstract "intelligence") that is expressed in the behavior of both species. In other words, we must not abstract "intelligence" from the ape infant and abstract "intelligence" from the human infant, and then compare them as though they were mere degrees and tempi of one phenomenon of "pure intelligence." The comparatively rapid development of ape intelligence is rooted in the distinct phylogeny of the ape, not of the human. The significance of this is ignored by investigators who are preoccupied with an abstract "mental ability." They overlook the fact that the psychogenetic potential of the human infant for learning its own culture is inborn and that this becomes increasingly apparent as the development of the two primates of distinct species are compared and observed side by side. Put simply, the actual behavior (not merely potential) of the human infant at only nine months of age is more advanced than any chimpanzee at the age of thirty!

The starting point of what is uniquely human in the behavior of the human baby is the smile. This smile expresses at once recognition, expectation, communication, and the need for an other. Baby chimpanzees and monkeys have many gestures, postures, facial expressions, and emotive sounds that express this need in their own way. But they have no behavioral equivalent for concentrating all the ingredients of this highly complex and emotional response, which Erik Erikson so aptly describes as hope, into one specific act of welcoming recognition, into what I call the Smile of Great Expectations. As Erikson has said, when the baby smiles at the human face the adult cannot help smiling back. Both adult and baby are filled with the expectations of a recognition that confirms their need for each other: "The fact is that the mutuality of adult and baby is the original source of hope, the basic ingredient of all effective as well as ethical human action."[1] It is true that the baby monkey Polly at the age of three weeks was making greeting gestures that expressed "hope" in her own way. These displays were a mixture of much head shaking and emotive sounds of *tuff tuff*, but the eyes were usually closed and the face expressionless.

It can also be said that monkeys laugh in their own way, but they do not laugh as humans do or for quite the same reasons. The juvenile monkey Charlie, for example, makes the characteristic lagothrix sound of *huh huh*, a strongly expelled or exhaled "chuckle." It is a very seductive and appealing sound, and it is always accompanied by a vigorous sideways shaking of the head. This sound and the head shaking can express numerous and conflicting elements of intention, and it is part of a complex of appeasement behavior and the invitation to play and fraternize. In adolescent behavior it fluctuates from extreme good humor to an ecstasy of aggressive pleasure. Beginning at the point of what I call "good intentions," the mouth is open and the lips are spread in an expression similar to that of the human laugh. Should the mood, however, develop in the direction of "aggressive ecstasy," the brows will contract and the eyes narrow, the mouth will open wider, and the head shaking will become more rapid and vigorous. This may occur in a play-fight between two dominant males that exceeds the limits of friendly rivalry, and it can be a very painful experience for the loser.

There is of course a highly sadistic element in most fun making and even in the most sophisticated forms of humor. We have all seen ourselves when laughing to excess, waving our arms about, screwing up the face muscles, tensing our lips, and even frowning as though we were in pain. Some of us are so skilled in the art of hiding our cruel intentions that we affect a laugh to cloak a jeer, perhaps at an opponent who is scoring heavily in an argument we are losing in bad grace. Our children will also laugh themselves into a frenzy of joy at the comic spectacle of an adult in distress, particularly when father discovers that "someone" has tipped the watering can upside down on his side of the bed. Clearly there is a psychological similarity between the monkey's aggressive chuckle of *huh huh* and human laughter.

The year-old monkey will chuckle, pull your nose, steal your glasses and your fountain pen and unscrew the cap, all in five seconds flat. This is beyond the physical ability and practical intelligence of the one-year-old human infant. But that same infant at the age of nine months draws upon a built-in sense of the incongruous, and of hope, expectation, and humor, that enables it to enjoy the subtlety of a game like Peep-Bo! The infant will laugh with excitement when the disappearing face reappears unexpectedly (and reassuringly) from behind the chair. The appreciation and response on this level of fun is incomprehensible to any ape or monkey regardless of its age. One can indeed play Peep-Bo with a young monkey or ape, but the face remains blank and one hears no emotive sounds of pleasure or joy. The "game" is one of curiosity and puzzlement only. Once understood, all interest comes to an end.

There is another level of humor, of empathetic projection, when the spectacle of another's misfortune appears both comic and pleasurable because the observer himself is not directly involved. A well-known classic in this form has been given by Stephen Leacock of two young Eskimos sitting by a crack in the ice, helpless with laughter, because their father had just slipped through it and disappeared from sight. The average child of eighteen months will also scream with delight when father plays the game of walking straight into a door by accident and pretending to be seriously injured. Such playacting may impress and interest a chimpanzee, but the animal will not be amused on the human level of comic discernment, even though a year-old chimpanzee can perform feats of skill impossible for a human infant of eighteen months.

A sense of humor in a human context, even on the level of Peep-Bo, is a sense of the incongruous, a dimension of cognition that is more significant than the ability to unscrew a lid from a jar, press a button for food, or turn on the tap for a drink of water. No chimpanzee is able to comprehend, initiate, and reenact the observed behavior of a human being in fantasy. I am thinking of those creative acts of "imitation" that are performed by any infant from eighteen months on. For example, our eldest son Samuel at the age of eighteen months was intrigued by the difficulties experienced by our handyman Harry in starting his motorcycle. One day after Harry had left, Samuel came into the house, climbed onto his tricycle, and reenacted Harry's entire ritual of frustration and foot stamping on the self-starter, including Harry's favorite terms of abuse. Nonhuman primates do not display that kind of intelligence, if indeed such creative behavior can be adequately described in the simple context of "intelligence."

Another favorite with children of eighteen months is the game of go-stop-go. The trick is to stop and go immediately on command and with military precision. The thrill and satisfaction experienced by the infant in the exercise of such power and push-button control is a joy to see. Infants will also enjoy throwing an object to the ground continuously, gurgling with pleasure as the object is replaced only to be seized and flung down again to the floor. The more distress affected by the parent during this "game," the more delighted the child will be. Another dimension of the power of innate expression is found in infant babble singing. Our youngest son Daniel at twenty months of age was singing "tunes" of two notes a minor third apart. It would not surprise me to learn that there are many infants who achieve this at a much earlier age, if only parents were able to recognize the significance of these early forms of musical feeling and innate sense of rhythm. At sixteen months of age Daniel could not light a match with the skill of a twelve-month-old chimpanzee, but he used to copy my ritual of shaving. He would also reenact the game of father banging his head on the door, and he was delighted when we applauded his performance and laughed with approval. In short, the chimpanzee is a wonderful animal and a born innovator, but the human child is a divine actor.

CHAPTER 9

Instinct for Continuity

For most anthropologists the concepts "savage" and "primitive" are abstractions of little use. They refer either to Paleolithic cultures about which very little is known or they are used incorrectly to describe existing preliterate or tribal cultures that are anything but prototypes of the so-called noble savage, nor can they be regarded as "primitive." Presumably the "man of nature" is no longer with us. His origin is either a mystery that corresponds with the mythology of the Fall, or it is represented by a break from the forest hominids in prehistory.

In a previous chapter I tried to show that the popular conception of "primitive" man as a "break" from nature in prehistory is a negative concept. The break was not a "biocultural leap," but a transitional stage of genetic and cultural change that was historically determined. Clearly a concept is required that approximates the nature of the men of that period. For want of a better concept I shall refer to these early races of men as aborigines to distinguish them from the precultures and preconscious levels of the early hominids and also from the successive races of men who followed them in the name of "civilized history." In this context "aboriginal culture" is represented in history as well as prehistory. The most exacting anthropologist must concede that the hunter-gatherer cultures of the Australian Aranda and Tiwi, the Tasmanians, the Congo Pygmies, and the Kalahari Bushmen must be distinguished from those tribal cultures in precolonial Africa and elsewhere that were already corrupted by slavery and class dominance long before they were invaded by the "Christian culture" of modern Europeans.

Communication and traffic between African and neighboring cultures has been taking place for at least three thousand years. The penetration and influence of Egyptian cultures on the tribes of East and central Africa is strongly evident in African art, particularly in music. The shapes of many African lyre-type instruments are strikingly similar to those of the ancient Egyptians. The *icilongo*, a bamboo trumpet used by the Zulus, has its prototype in the ancient Roman *Lituus*, and flutes similar in type to the Zulu *umtshingo* were also used in ancient Egypt. The *nai* of the present-day Arabs is virtually the same instrument. The technique of the old Egyptian flutes was also similar to the Zulu *umtshingo*, a three-holed flute that undoubtedly influenced the instrumental techniques and the development of the heptatonic scale in African music.[1]

The invasion of more complex cultures also brought new techniques for economic exploitation, war, and the enslavement of women and children. Natural rites became overritualized and institutionalized into dogma, enabling patriarchal hierarchies with the help of political shamans to rule with an authority as oppressive as any found among our modern industrial states. Iris Andreski writes:

The type of sexual segregation practised by most West African peoples was a necessary factor in the production of efficient militaristic units linked together by chains of terrorist "secret societies," whose aim was the maintenance of a small privileged elite and the subjugation of a proletariat of women, children and slaves.[2]

Clearly a distinction must be made between the aboriginal cultures that are closer to nature and those of the tribal peoples of precolonial Africa. The distinction is also important for the theme of the present chapter, the instinct for continuity, by which I mean the instinct for the unity of historical and concrete knowledge that characterizes the life of the aborigine. Existing hunter-gatherer peoples are no more "primitive," in the archaic sense of the early hominids, than the so-called literate peoples, yet many psychologists have compared the emotional and mental life of the adult savage with that of a European child of an industrial culture. This has led to the fallacy that the language and thought of tribal peoples is deficient in concepts and lacking in precision and system. Kretschmer says "the thought of primitive peoples allows of but little arrangement and condensation of separate images into abstract categories." Koestler supports this view when he says that the language of the "primitive" and of the child is "like the unfolding of a picture-strip; each word expresses a picture, regardless of whether it signifies an object or an action."[3]

Abstract words are not in fact the monopoly of "civilized" languages. The Tasmanians distinguished between past, present, and future, and Franz Boas tells us that in Chinook language the proposition "The bad man killed the poor child" is expressed "The man's badness killed the child's poverty." For "The woman used too small a basket" the Chinook say, "She put the potentilla roots into the smallness of a clam basket."[4] Lévi-Strauss reminds us that the savage forms concepts in accordance with his needs and that his language is rich in precise knowledge as well as in general ideas:

Words like "oak," "beech," "birch" etc., are not less entitled to be considered as abstract words than the word "tree"; and a language possessing only the word "tree" would be from this point of view less rich in concepts than o..e which lacked this term but contained dozens or hundreds for individual species and varieties.[5]

The Tamanac tribes have abstract words for grandeur, envy, and lightness. Concept and reality are welded together in the following words: fingers (*amgnamucura*) = "the sons of the hand," mushrooms (*jeje-panari*) = "the ears of a tree," leaves (*prutpe-jareri*) = "the hair at the top of the tree," thunder (*adotsa*) = "the noise of the cloud." The Chaymas say that the moon is "another earth." Years are counted by the number of winters or rain seasons, and in Chayma they say, "so many rains." Concepts are strengthened with action and color in the language of the Lengua Indians; for "I am hungry" they say,

"I am killed with hunger" and for "I am cold," "I am perished with the south wind." Concepts for the emotions are seated in the chest: courage = strong chest, desire = dead chest, agony = moving chest. Verbs are inflected for qualification by affixes: *yintim-anteyi* = to lead here, *yintim-akme* = to lead to a distant place.[6] Instead of saying "The food was given to us by our forefathers," the Kwakiutl Indians say, "The food here is the goodwill of our forefathers." For "This is my name" they say, "This is the weight of my name." "You are robbing your parents" is expressed "You are making your parents poor." Concept and emotion mingle in phrases like "We will make soft inside with our songs."[7]

In my view the "single word" could never have been the starting point of any language any more than the single note could have been the starting point of music. According to the convincing theory of John Rowbotham, early chant music began not with original "notes," but with compressed phrases. The Maoris, for example, do not always sing one clear note and then another, passing from note to note in the making of their phrases; each note in many of their older chant-songs is a phrase in itself.

If we accept this Maori phrase as in reality one phrase-note, it may be compared with the sentence-word *Nikmiktia*, which is

Nahuatl for "I kill it," or with the ancient Mexican word *Nischotshitemoa*, "gather flowers." I believe that the word in language has had the same history as the note in music,[8]

This may account for the survival of "meaningless words" in the songs of many tribal peoples. The ethnomusicologist Charles Myers writes: "The cause of meaningless words in primitive songs lies in the antiquity of the music. The words become so archaic, or their sense was originally so involved or symbolical that all meaning gradually disappears as the song is handed down from generation to generation."[9] Strong support for this explanation is found in Florence Densmore's study of Chippewa music:

Minute graduation of tone in Indian song has given rise to the statement that the Chippewa Indians habitually use intervals of eighths and quarter tones. It is the opinion of this writer that these minutely graded tones are survivals of a less differentiated vocal expression. In Indian Chippewa music we observe the tones on which a purely natural vocal expression crystallizes and first coincides with that system of tones which had gradually developed in the musical history of the white race.[10]

There are many intellectuals in our modern society who are skilled in the art of semantics but alarmingly ignorant of a mass of experiences and a knowledge of concrete things in the living world. The aborigine, with his inexhaustible knowledge of the plant and animal kingdom, and the fusion of this knowledge with his art, religion, and labor, has little need of concepts that have no bearing on his life. Although he has a thirst for knowledge of the facts in his environment, he nevertheless looks for unity, authenticity, and order in everything. A strik-

ing example of how the elements of history and science combine in the savage mind is provided in Polynesian mythology:

Fire and water married, and from them sprung the earth, rocks,
trees, and everything. The cuttlefish fought with the fire and was
beaten. The fire fought with the rocks, and the rocks conquered.
The large stones fought with the small stones; the small ones conquered. The trees fought with the creepers, the trees were beaten
and the creepers conquered. The creepers rotted, swarmed with
maggots, and from maggots they grew to be men.[11]

The botanical and zoological knowledge of the savage is no
less orderly than that of the most exacting taxonomist. The
Pinatubo Negritoes can distinguish the habits of fifteen species
of bats and a phenomenal number of plants, insects, and birds.
On the culture of the Kabiran people we read:

Even a child can frequently identify the kind of tree from which
a tiny wood fragment has come and, furthermore, the sex of that
tree, as defined by Kabiran notions of plant sex, by observing the
appearance of its wood and bark, its smell, its hardness, and similar
characters. Fish and shellfish by the dozen are known by individually distinctive terms, and their separate features and habits
as well as the sexual difference within each type, are well recognized.[12]

The savage respects and laments the dead, but in his poetry life
and death are interwoven in the theme of the living. His instinct for continuity is even humorously expressed in a sexual
realism that persists in the face of death. This is made very
clear in a song of the Australian Euahlayi tribe, in which the
conflict between lust and death is resolved in favor of survival.
In this song a woman speaks at the graveside of her dead
husband, who has been killed by another man. She appeases his
violent death, but at the same time prepares herself for the
erotic advance of her husband's murderer:

Let us sit down together,
We'll stay here, no matter how hot the sun.
It was by the mango-tree that he shot you;
Close to your father's grave at Partarapu.
I have plenty of hair between my legs,
And that man's going to grab me.[13]

Nowhere is the rhythmic unity of thought and feeling so clearly expressed as in the chant and dance ritual of the savage. The contrapuntal rhythms of African music in particular display an astonishing imagination as well as technical control. In the Bamba dance there are four drum rhythms, each with its own point of entry, so staggered that the different rhythms cross one another. The Australian Arnhem Land aborigines possess a remarkable polyrhythmic sense. The figure on p. 89[14] illustrates the main rhythmic patterns by sticks and didjeridoo that occur in the accompaniment of one of their chant songs. The rhythmic virtuosity of the playing is of such a high order that the syncopated figures produced by the upper note can be read as a separate part. The melody consists of five chanting notes on the scale shown on the next page.

When we consider the natural inclination of the savage both to generalize and specialize in unity, it is difficult to sympathize with those missionaries who complained of the difficulty in introducing Christian concepts to tribal peoples. Barbrook Grubb complained about the patience that is required for explaining symbols and imagery to the "primitive mind" when everything is likely to be taken literally. Unconscious of the humor of his "difficulty," he wrote:

I was exhibiting a lantern slide of the Twelve Apostles to the Chaco Indians, and it was impossible to explain that it was an imaginary group. I had to name them individually. . . . On seeing a picture of an angel they puzzled over it for a long time, and eventually remarked: "How can he use his wings—they spring from the backbone instead of the shoulder?" It was a hard task to make it clear that angelic wings were only symbolical.[15]

Barbrook Grubb ran into more trouble when he built a church hut in which the congregation was not allowed to smoke. When reprimanded, an offender covered his head with a blanket as though to take a nap, and smoke was seen later rising through the blanket. Cautioned again, the Indian said, "I did not think the spirit would see me." The same Indian, with the dignity of a wider knowledge, would persist in saying at the end of his prayer "Goodnight" instead of "Amen."

Ex.1²

The humor of the difficulties experienced by the conscientious missionary wears very thin when one considers the destructive effects of a Christian culture on the indigenous cultures of the Amazon Indians. The systematic extermination of the forest tribes of Brazil continues as I write, and it is here that we find the white man's "instinct for discontinuity" violating all the laws of the living.

Among the few remaining Indian tribes, the Maxacali are protected by a constitution that in theory gives them possession of their ancestral land, but powerful landowning groups known as *facendas* have cleared the forests and narrowed boundaries so that the Indians can no longer hunt and fish. When the state police in 1967 reclaimed 7,000 acres and provided every Maxacali family with one cow, within six months the tribe was self-supporting, producing a surplus in milk and cheese as well as in handicrafts. Recent reports show that the *facendas* with the help of white missionaries are continuing to destroy indigenous cultures by venal trafficking. One party of university students on a field study in the Mato Grosso found only hunger and exploitation. In March 1968 the Brazilian government admitted that, despite the efforts of the Indian protectorate, the forest Indians were on the verge of extinction. An official report exposed the atrocities committed by corrupt politicians and landowners in which whole tribes had been destroyed by bacteriological warfare and the poisoning of food. Of 19,000 Munducurus known to be alive in the 1930s, only 1,200 are left today; and of 10,000 Cinta largus, who were attacked from the air, only 500 have survived. It is estimated that only 100,000 Indians of all tribes survive today, and Darci Ribeiro, Brazil's leading authority on the forest Indians, has produced a statistical survey which indicates that not a single Indian will be left in the Brazilian forests by 1980.[16]

While the extermination of the Indian cultures continues, the missionaries continue to express astonishment at the failure of the savage mind to understand the virtues of ownership, chastity, and the Christian Hereafter. In an interview with Quentin Crewe, the explorer David Smithers said:

The missionaries build a church, which creates a village, with the result that tribes who are accustomed to roaming freely settle in villages and within a month the area is hunted out. Forced to wear clothes, they catch diseases and become ravaged by skin complaints. Missionaries complain that if the Indians were not dressed the rubber workers would lust after them. One evangelist referred to the difficulty of explaining the "next world" to savages who already believe that they live in two worlds. A native with tears in his eyes said he could not be a Christian: "My father never heard the message and so he must be in Hell. I want to be with him when I die." Another priest complained that the Indians had no pride in personal possessions. "Do you know," he said, "a man may spend a whole month making a bow, and along comes someone who admires the bow and the man will give it to him!"[17]

With the concept of "foreign aid for the underdeveloped peoples" comes a new stage in the white man's talent for hypocrisy and rape. Immediately a so-called underdeveloped people are trapped in a capitalist economy, they lose their native art and skills in return for industrial wages to buy guns, bullets, cigarettes, European clothes, and a photograph of the royal family; meanwhile the new technological predator devours their homeland and their natural resources. Seduced by the affluency of the Western style of living, the aborigines crowd the "development areas" where they reproduce all the symptoms and poverty of "underdevelopment." This is what happened to the Australian aborigines, and it is precisely what is happening today in New Guinea, where the Australian government's "good neighbor" policy provides "education" and "economic assistance" to the "underdeveloped" New Guinea tribes, who never suffered from "underdevelopment" until the white Australians inflicted it upon them.

In our de-instinctualized Western society of overdevelopment and false affluence we are educated to believe that our natural sense organs are narrow windows through which to perceive the world. To explore the world of the miniature and to see distant objects our inborn senses must be supplemented by the instruments of science. Unfortunately, man's insatiable desire for freedom from the limitations of his natural senses is being pursued at the cost of losing them. Our survival is already comparable with the sterilized existence of a desocialized ape in a zoo. Such an animal displays none of the primordial magnificence and dignity of the natural ape in his own habitat. Nevertheless, the zoo ape is able to survive and reproduce, not as a living animal, but as an anatomical representative of his species. A similar prospect faces man in his ability to adapt and survive in a decultured limbo. G. K. Chesterton said: "A man is a slave until he is no longer a slave." Pasteur demonstrated the same principle by placing a bird in a closed cage and conditioning it to air pollution by gradual changes in the quality of air. When another unconditioned bird was placed suddenly into the same cage it died immediately.

The tragedy of our time is not only the energy crisis but the loss of our instinct for continuity and the possibility that man will succeed in adapting to an automated existence, to an anti-culture which has exiled all the spiritual, aesthetic, and biological impulses that constitute the very drive and fabric of human nature. In such an environment words like *humanity, beauty, kinship, love,* and *art* will have no meaning. If a human environment is to have any meaning, it must express the fundamental nature of man. His deepest biological rhythms and impulses are rooted in the seasons; in soil, water, trees, and grass; and in his universal kinship with nature's inherent morality of love and need for an other. To forget this is to make a god of reason and to repeat Hegel's error when he said: "So long as love and sympathy are instinctive, as with the man of nature, their universality of scope is corrupted by self-seeking action."

When the explorer Robert Burke was dying from starvation and scurvy in the Australian desert, he refused gifts of food from the friendly aborigines. He recorded in his diary that he would never suffer the indignity of accepting help from the heathen savages. In this situation it would be proper to ask Hegel who was guilty of "corrupted self-seeking action," Burke or the men of nature. If Hegel were alive today I would also ask him what kind of world he would like to see growing in the hearts of our children: a "democratic" power structure that now wants to conquer the universe or the one of our own earth, illuminated with the insights of the man of nature:

The Aranda native sees recorded in the surrounding landscape the ancient story of the lives and the deeds of the immortal beings whom he reveres; beings, many of whom he has known in his own experiences as fathers, grandfathers and brothers, and as his mothers and sisters. The whole countryside is his living, age-old family tree; the story of his own doings at the beginning of time, and at the dawn of life, when the world as he knows it now was being shaped and moulded by all-powerfull hands.[19]

It is true that an aboriginal culture, like all cultures, must defend itself against an environment that is hostile as well as friendly. But in tribal life the enemies are appeased as spirits of the unknown who threaten the health and survival of all individuals in the tribe. In political terms the fundamental difference between the traditional taboos imposed in aboriginal society and the ideology of our technological power structure is that the latter define the "enemy" in terms of their own interests and then conscript people to fight for those interests regardless of the threat to human life as a whole. I am not suggesting that we can rejoin the nature we are exiling by returning to the tribal life of our ancestors. With my own incurable optimism I nevertheless believe that we shall find a way of pulling back the mad rush for technological expansion and that a day will come when the example of the aborigine will help us to regain the instinct for continuity we seem to have lost.

CHAPTER 10

Beauty and the Beast

The truth that one man's culture can be another man's poison is illustrated by Humboldt in an anecdote on the cannibalism practiced by the Caribs of the Orinoco:

The natives carried off a Dominican monk from the coast of Porto Rico and devoured him. They all fell sick and said they would never again eat a monk. The monks were horrified at what they called the perversity of the Indian race; one old missionary said: "You receive a man from a new tribe into the village and he appears to be mild, good and intelligent, and then to your horror you discover on talking to him that he prefers the flesh of monkeys because it has the same taste as human flesh. In his eyes it is no more unjust to kill and eat his enemies than it is to hunt the jaguar. Only a sense of propriety induces him to eat the same food as ourselves at the mission."[1]

A comparative study with King Leopold II of the Belgians would show that the Guaisian Indian was indeed highly moral. Leopold himself shot 700 gorillas in one year for sport, and his regime of "economic development" in the Congo cost the lives of 8 million black people. Old documents and photographs still exist, showing men strung up on a line with hands and feet amputated because they stole from Leopold's estate. No savage culture could afford the luxury of such crimes as these.

In the magico-ritual of the Haida tribe of North American Indians, cannibalism was confined to slaves captured in war or to the corpses of deceased relatives. Viewed historically, these seemingly bizarre customs were rooted in the social traditions and moral life of the savage, and if our own moral sense rebels it is only because it expels a custom that offends the traditional norms of our own culture. As recently as 100 years ago an eyewitness of a totemic ceremony of the North American Haida tribe wrote:

A female slave was asked to dance in the hamatsa ceremony. Before she began she said: "Do not get hungry, do not eat me." She had hardly said so when her master, who was standing beside her, split her skull with an axe, and she was eaten by the hamatsa. . . . Besides devouring slaves, the hamatsas also devour corpses. . . . After initiation a new hamatsa will sometimes return from the woods carrying a corpse, which is eaten after the dance. The skin is cut around the wrist and ankles, as they must not eat the hands and feet, else they believe they would die immediately. . . . The bear-dancers cut the bodies of slaves and, growling like bears, give pieces to the highest hamatsa first and then to the others. The bones are then tied up and thrown into the river, in the belief that they would return and take their master's soul.[2]

Clearly a parallel to the secret societies and overritualized ceremonies of the warlike Haida tribes is found in the type of sexual segregation and terrorist societies existing in precolonial Africa. Such cultures cannot be taken as typical of those indigenous cultures represented by the peace-loving Aranda and Tiwi tribes of Australia, or the Kabirans, the Samoans, the Kalahari Bushmen, the Congo Pygmies, and the Eskimo Aleuts. Even so, Franz Boas has shown that the original rites of the Haida tribes evolved into theatrical ceremonies in which there was no killing or even biting and tearing of the flesh; they merely pulled the skin with their teeth. In one of these ceremonies the speaker says:

"Let us tame our friends, else we cannot eat in peace." They then sing the song which tames the bears: "Great is the fury of the Supernatural One. He will carry men on his arms and torment them. He will devour them skin and bones." After the song the speaker says: "How beautiful I have been made by the Supernatural One. I shall give dried salmon to all of us."[3]

Those who like to think of the original rites as immoral in the abstract and for all cultures should remember that similar "barbarous customs" were practiced by the Egyptians in the thirteenth century:

Snares were set for physicians by people who pretended to be sick, but were only hungry. The physicians were called not to be consulted, but to be devoured. The practice spread into the provinces and was adopted everywhere. People of wealth and respectability ate human flesh as their ordinary food, even to lay in a stock of it. The mania of devouring one another became so common among the poor that the greater number of them perished in this manner.[4]

Leonardo da Vinci expressed his moral indignation in an address to the medieval cannibals of his time:

If you are, as you have described yourselves, the king of animals, it would be better for you to call yourselves the king of beasts, since you are the greatest of them all. . . . This supreme form of wickedness hardly exists among the animals, except among those species which sometimes eat their young. But not only do you eat your children, you eat father, mother, brother, and friends, and this even not sufficing, you make raids on foreign lands and capture men and women of other races and cram them down your gullets.[5]

A well-known case of cannibalism that is closer to our own time is quoted by Iwan Bloch:

Sawney Beane was born in East Lothian in the times of James i. He was the son of an honest hedger and ditcher, who withdrew with an idle and profligate woman into a cave on the sea-coast in the wilds of Galloway. She lived with him for twenty-five years in this hiding place and produced eight sons and six daughters. The whole family lived as cannibals on the flesh of human beings whom they ambushed or lured into the cave, murdered and dismembered, cooked, roasted and pickled like dried beef. When these cave dwellers were at last arrested the cave was full of salted and dried human meat dangling from the roof.[6]

From the texts we have considered, it is easy to look back with horror and despair at man's history as one of cruelty and massacre. In our own time this picture of man's inhumanity has produced a crop of negative theories on the ontology of the so-called destructive psyche; a collection of hybrid concepts in which life, health, and love have been equated with death, sickness, and hate in such fictions as the "life-death instinct," the "love-hate drive," and in the biological concept of the "pain-pleasure syndrome." In the chapter "Aggression" I considered how the polarities of love and hate and of pleasure and pain will never be understood while their subnormal and pathological forms are confused with their positive function in the natural preservation of the species. It is when the individual animal fails to relate successfully with its society that "pain" is often preferred, not to "pleasure," but to frustration. Whether this frustration is determined by the pathology of the individual or the stresses of a sick society, whether in fact it is socially conditioned or self-imposed, must be the subject of a later chapter. Here I am concerned with the error of interpreting man's potential for cruelty as a negative and destructive instinct, genetically determined by the adoption of a carnivorous diet and the lycanthropic (wolflike) habits of the so-called murderous and jealous predator. Following is a classic form of this error:

We are all descended from males of the carnivorous lycanthropic (wolf) variety, a mutation evolved under the pressure of hunger caused by climatic change at the end of the pluvial period, which induced indiscriminate, even cannibalistic, predatory aggression, culminating in the rape and sometimes in the devouring of the females.[7]

My first objection to the concept of man as "a mutation from the passive anthropoid to lycanthropic man" is that it gives an entirely inaccurate picture of the functional behavior of predatory animals like the wolf and the lion. As we saw in chapter 5, it would be more accurate to contrast the passive cat with the pathogenic ape. Second, the old idea of the predatory primate hunter overlooks the creditable features of hunting as a way of life. The development of the aesthetic sense depended on a hunting culture. The importance of balance, speed, and power in the making of new tools and weapons required more symmetry, smoothness, and beauty of line. Selection pressures also favored those hunters who hit the game with more efficiency: "It is no accident that the bones of small-brained men (Australopithecus) are never found with beautiful, symmetrical tools . . . clearly the success of tools has exerted a great influence on the evolution of the brain and has created skills that made art possible."[8]

Human hunters depend on an intimate knowledge of large areas. A small community of Bushmen requires a hunting territory of several hundred square miles and a number of waterholes for support, but a comparative number of baboons can be supported by an area of a few square miles and one waterhole. The hunting way of life therefore produces a greater knowledge of animal and plant life and new techniques and skills, particularly with regard to sharing, division of labor, care of children, and the growing consciousness of the importance of group solidarity. The killing of large animals such as the rhinoceros and bear must have required highly cooperative action, and there is no doubt that hunting also nurtured the development of mutual aid and comradeship.

The powerful effect of the hunting way of life on human psychology, particularly with regard to intraspecific aggression, is not in dispute. It is clear to see in modern man's love of killing as a sport and in the enthusiasm of children for war and killing games. But this interest is both encouraged and developed in a modern society that is itself obsessed with competition. The fundamental relationship of the Kalahari Bushmen with the animals of Africa was never one of hunter and hunted: "He knew the animal and vegetable life of Africa as they have never been known since . . . . He seemed to know what it actually felt like to be a lion, an elephant or an antelope. The proof is there in his paintings on his beloved rocks for those who can see with their hearts as well as their eyes."[9] The Eskimo Aleuts train their boys in the skill of throwing harpoons with accuracy and power while seated in kayaks, but the emotional machinery that supplies the energy for this action is not comparable with the destructive behavior of the modern child who rushes around the streets of suburbia mowing down people with a toy machine gun.

It is also wrong to compare the violence of delinquents in our society with the aggressive play-fighting that is encouraged in juvenile monkeys by the adult males. Dominant males in the monkey group are actively engaged and equally responsible for encouraging and developing the inhibitory controls for appeasement and friendship. This social education is not only the responsibility of the females. Male instruction occurs during competitive play as well as in situations that are fraternal and peaceful. We considered earlier how these instinctual displays form part of a complex system of social communication and that the head-shaking gesture of greeting and appeasement by infant monkeys is self-motivated.

In the chapter "The Birth of Sin" we saw that the conflict between self-interest and group unity in man leads to a specific dilemma for which no true paradigm exists among nonhuman primates. To explain this dilemma in terms of "the murderous predator," the "pleasure-pain" principle, or in abstractions like the "life-death" instinct is to treat the human psyche as though it were a pathological entity at constant war with the social nature of man. This confusion is fundamental in Freudian theory: "All the dangerous and ugly impulses which we are struggling against stand nearer to nature than do our resistances to them." As I have indicated, it would be closer to the truth to say that our resistance to the pathological violence of modern man is rooted in an instinctual morality for mutual cooperation, in a social instinct that is fundamental in all primate societies. But this simple truth has only the ring of oversimplification for those who fail to distinguish between the healthy function of creative individuality and the obsessional neuroses of the Western mind.

A number of psychologists are now considering the therapeutic value of Eastern mysticism for sedating the obsessional drives of "Christian rationalism." This has produced its own cult in the expanding literature and practice of Buddhist psychiatry. The Freudian superego is now being retailored to fit the Eastern concept of a transcendental absolute, "timeless being," or "nonself" that is in conflict with the instinctual ego in much the same way as the latter is repressed by the self or "conscious I." It is another way of establishing a new balance of power in favor of an abstract universal, another way of sedating the natural drives of individuals who may otherwise rebel against the mass neurosis of a sick establishment.

Neither can the surrender of individuality in the "death instinct" of Eastern religion be compared with that instinct for continuity that characterizes the life of tribal man. Where Anglo-Saxon "Christian intellectualism" has dogmatized culture, Eastern mysticism has renounced it altogether. Observers have described how individuals in the East will offer no resistance to disease, how they will even commit suicide in the absence of any explicit reason or cause for doing so: "The relative immunity of the white races in areas in the East exposed to pandemics, may be due to the fact that the death impulse in them is less strong . . . . I think one would be quite safe in saying that the high death roll from infections in the East is associated with the high incidence of the death wish."[10] The "death wish" may also be a serviceable concept for explaining the attraction of war for neurotics who have lost their social identity in peacetime, as long as its pathology is recognized in contrast with the "health instinct" of those who do not require the mass neurosis of war to give a point to their lives or to inspire heroics. In this context, it is not the so-called affluence of our welfare state that generates violence and a destructive attitude to life. The "death wish" in so many of our young people who are impelled to flirt with death, whether in gang war, crime, or by dying on their motorcycles, is a pathological reaction to the absence of real ties with a creative culture. If all that is meant by the "death wish" is that death is sometimes preferred to life, then we have known that for a long time, but only because death in its proper context has already been accepted as the servant of the living. Disregarding the positive aspects of death as a sacrifice to the living and taking it—as we are intended to, by our Buddhist-psychiatrists —as an instinctual escape from the "unbearable," then our "life instinct" will insist upon regarding the "unbearable" as the enemy and not abstractions like the "death wish."

"The "pathological psyche" is not the mainspring of the

primate ego; it signifies the failure of a sick animal to integrate successfully with its society. Neither is the pleasure-pain syndrome the operator of a paradoxical duality or a built-in sadomasochism; its function is subservient to the emotional needs of the group, with which individual creativity must identify. Although individual creativity must advance beyond the immediate economic and emotional needs of the group, its success will nevertheless depend on whether the advance (whether a new technique or a new philosophy) has a potential and not too distant value for new needs that are fundamentally social.

The biology of pain and pleasure cannot disclose the distinct nature of conflict in the human psyche simply because pain and pleasure are somatic sensations that do not and cannot enlighten us on the spiritual needs of the human primate. When the pleasure-pain principle is used to express a general theory of the evolution of motivational behavior, it degenerates into a form of "biological pragmatism" of no value for a rigorous science and philosophy of primate evolution. For example, it is common knowledge that biological pain is a signal of failure in the organism to achieve individual satisfaction, but as such it cannot explain the psychological significance of the "pleasure" of witnessing suffering through what I call social empathy. The erotic stimulation caused by the "lover's pinch which hurts but is desired" is as well known to the Amazon monkey Jessy as it is to the Amazon Queen in Kleist's tragedy *Penthesilea;* but Jessy does not express her empathy with the suffering of others on the pathogenic level of the Amazon Queen, who joined her pack of wild dogs in biting and tearing the flesh of her victim Achilles. Jessy nevertheless is capable of empathetic participation in the spectacle of pain inflicted on others when that empathy is rooted in group security. This is clearly illustrated in the behavior of our lagothrix colony, who love to participate (at a safe distance) in the dramatic behavior of outsiders.

Pandemonium reigns in the monkey community whenever a mock battle is staged between our wolfhound dogs and myself. In the desire to lend moral support the monkeys will scream with excitement, jump up and down, slash ropes, and throw objects about, just as human spectators at a sporting event will chant, stamp, and throw their hats in the air. Tension reaches even greater heights when we chase the donkeys away from the borders of monkey territory. This event is supported by a chorus of monkey abuse and aggressive displays of intimidation. The social content of the situation is clear: in the eyes of the monkey, donkeys are strange animals who appear to be totally unresponsive to social signals of threat that would command the respect of any wild and natural animal. Add to this the unknown danger suggested by their size and their eccentric habit of occasionally walking backward while feeding on grass, and it is easy to understand why the monkeys are delighted and stimulated by a mock attack that they naturally assume is performed for their benefit.

Such empathy and participation is not pathological; it would be better described as moral support for a victor who manhandles large and dangerous-looking intruders who represent a threat to group security. We are in no way enlightened on the functional significance of such behavior by explaining its psychological significance in terms of somatic pleasure derived from watching or even participating in the cruelty inflicted on others. Equally futile is the attempt to interpret the intraspecific cruelty and "innate jealousy" of man as an atavistic throwback to the hunting instinct of the so-called murderous predator.

Another variation on the theme of "the beast in man" is the claim that "love is a destructive impulse for devouring as well as for copulation." We know well the relation between eating and copulation. Lévi-Strauss refers to the Yoruba language in which "to eat" and "to marry" are expressed by a single verb, a usage that has a parallel in the French word *consommer*, which applies to both meals and marriage. The word *Huta Kuta* in *Koto Yoa* means both incest and cannibalism, and in African Matabele the word *totem* also means "sister's vulva," an indirect confirmation of the relation between eating and copulation.[11] But this kind of evidence is not supposed to support the concept of love as an emotion at war with itself. It should be obvious that the impulse to bite, eat, smell, pinch, and claw *must* be rooted in the emotive physiology of the mating and sexual instinct. If the sexual drive did not draw its energy and sensory satisfaction from its own biology, lovers would be ghosts instead of human beings.

Similar confusions persist in Freud's concept of the "self-assertive ego of animalism" and in Jung's "dark forces of the unconscious." The element of truth in these concepts overlooks the fact that our resistance to an "unconscious amorality" also stems from an instinctual and unconscious premorality. This has already been taken up in chapter 5. A closer look, however, at the relationship between the conscious mind and the unconscious will prepare the way for the chapter that follows.

Almost all great scientists, poets, and philosophers have said that verbal thinking played a subordinate role in their creative work and that their most revolutionary discoveries depended on visual and auditory intuitions which took shape spontaneously in the imagery of the subconscious. Goethe said: "Man cannot persist long in the conscious state. He must throw himself back into the unconscious, for his root is there." When Willa Muir was asked how the poet Edwin Muir worked, she said: "He waited for the dream, which might come one fragment at a time, until it was completed. And then he used his extremely active and competent intellect to revise and perfect it."

All of us to some extent think in images as well as concepts, alternating between the two levels of reason and instinct, of logic and intuition. But in the creative work of the artist and scientist this intuition is an intuitive understanding of the individual's own subject, experience, and work. It is not daydreaming, nor is it an intuition that is in conflict with the disciplines of a trained mind. In his criticism of the book *The Double Helix* C. H. Waddington makes a clear distinction between the disciplines of laboratory work and the faculty of intuitive understanding:

The actual "creative process" by which the DNA "breakthrough" was achieved does not in my opinion rank very high as scientific creation goes. . . . Watson approached DNA as though it were a super-complex jigsaw puzzle . . . this demands very high intelligence, but it is not the sort of operation involved in such major scientific advances as Darwin's theory of evolution, Einstein's relativity or Planck's quantum theory. And one is struck by how little Watson used a faculty which usually plays a large part in scientific discovery, namely intuitive understanding of the material. Of course, intuition can be drastically wrong, but it is usually a strong guide in innovative thinking.[12]

The paradox of two levels of the mind is often presented as though the human mind had been designed to remain a paradox. Clearly the failure to integrate the conflicting levels of the conscious and the unconscious can be disastrous for the human personality, but this does not mean that reason and the unconscious are continually at war. We are told, for example, that a repression of the autonomous demands of the unconscious may lead to a neurosis or that if we allow the "primitive emotions" to leap out, unrestrained by the disciplines of the conscious mind, we invite chaos and madness; or if we consciously guide and groom the imagery and emotive power of the unconscious then the value and spontaneity of the creative act is censored and irretrievably lost. As though the emotions were real and significant only for so long as they remained unconscious! Or that conscious thinking can take place only at the cost of alienation from the phylogenetic drives of the older mind!

The conscious level of the mind is not simply a ruthless censor whose sole function is to inhibit the creative and spontaneous drives of the older mind. The distinct levels of the conscious and the unconscious are also continuous, otherwise there would be no such thing as an individual. The creative mind does not renounce conceptual and productive thought, though it may well escape the tyranny of old mental habits and conventional disciplines that stand in the way of revolutionary discovery and advance. A great mind finds itself in harmony as well as conflict with a spontaneous source of powerful imagery, and those with smaller minds and smaller hearts will not find the inspirations of a Newton or a Rembrandt by returning to the dreams of their childhood or by giving unbridled expression to desires and passions that override a sense of moral responsibility to others. It is true that the creative act is also aggressive and compulsive, but for this reason the creative individual does not rely entirely upon the free play of the unconscious. When he retreats to the older levels of visual and sound imagery, he does not return with the fantasies of his childhood or with the hallucinations of a neurotic, but with images and intuitions that have been captured by a mature mind and transformed into creative acts on an adult level.

By dwelling on the negative aspects of human personality, it has been easy for a number of uncreative psychiatrists to analyze exceptional people in the arts as pathological types who failed to achieve the normal love relationships experienced by the common man. In this way Beethoven has been described as a schizoid personality "who never succeeded in making a permanent relationship with a woman."[13] The "diagnosis" is based on the stock-in-trade concepts of Freudian psychology, such as the "love-hate conflict in the infant psyche," or "maternal deprivation." It is understandable that the image of the philosopher for the nonphilosophical mind is that of a detached entity occupied with the creation of an ideal world. Presumably the creative thought of such philosophers as Socrates, Plato, Jesus, Kant, Hegel, Marx, and Sartre is also rooted in "maternal deprivation." If there were a grain of truth in this the facts of history would suggest that our present society is in need of *more* "maternal deprivation."

Hegel seems to have had the same problem with psychologists 150 years ago:

These psychologists are particularly fond of contemplating peculiarities in the character of great historical figures, as though everything they had accomplished were done under the impulse of some morbid craving. . . . Hence the conclusion follows that the ordinary man has no such passions, as though the proof did not already exist in that he does not accomplish anything great. . . . Great men do not derive their vocation from the regular course of things sanctioned by the existing order . . . they draw the impulse of their life from themselves. They are great because they *will* something great.[14]

When creative work is treated as a substitute for sexual and emotional frustration, we could as easily say that the normal man substitutes his normality for art or that the normal psychiatrist compensates for his lack of artistic feeling in his sex life. Psychology is a poor science when it confuses the relationship between human needs and frustrations with the creative urge in man for aesthetic experience, an impulse that functions spontaneously and independently of any "frustration neurosis." When the psychiatrist treats the impulse for aesthetic experience as a "frustration-compulsion" he is guilty of the same error as the behaviorist who explains aggression as simply a reaction to stress.

What creative people of distinction do possess is the power and the ability to express their feelings and their needs on psychological levels that are beyond the reach of many, but this does not mean that they are escapists who have alienated themselves from the world of the living. Many indeed are more involved with their personal relationships and their love and duties to their families than the so-called normal man. Clearly, intuition is autonomous, not a selected or consciously determined state of mind. But intuitions and intuition are not one and the same thing. Aggression, for example, is compulsive and autonomous, but how we aggress differs from one individual to another, and, what is more important, the individual himself has some control and therefore freedom over the character and the objectives of a variety of aggressive acts. The distinction I am making is highly significant when we are considering the content of specific emotional, aesthetic, and moral intuitions. Intuition as a dimension of the subconscious is compulsive, but the images of intuition are nevertheless evoked and characterized by the selective agency of a conditionally free and creative operator or initiator. I do not call this operator the conscious I, because concepts like the ego and superego invite a false dualism and not a valid or integrated polarity in the dynamics of the psyche. The older mind is both compulsive and predisposed to health and survival, indeed it insists on survival, but the images and insights that flash into consciousness are frequently triggered off or "invited" by the emotional, rational, and moral character of the operator, which I call the ethical self. The reason why we sometimes capture an image or an insight in our dream life that offers a solution to a problem or a dilemma is because we were already searching for that kind of solution. That is why these intuitive insights are so often welcome; when they do emerge one feels so elated and inspired that one may even look down on the conscious intellect as though it were a computer that had been programmed for IQ tests and spiritual death.

In this context we are not being tyrannized by the dogma of the conscious or by the phylogenetic persistence of the subconscious; we are being helped or enlightened by the ethical self, by what has been called the inner voice. If, however, the intuitive image we require is inhibited by guilt or deception, then the older mind (which I take as a species morality) will be in conflict with the conscious mind, and to that extent the guilt-resisting "unethical self" is already on the doorstep of the pathological. The images may then break through as hostile intruders in the form of distorted symbols or archetypes that are in conflict with the conscious mind. Jung's dream analyses are full of such examples.

Jung was concerned about what he called the deprivation by science and by Protestantism of man's "spiritual safeguards and means of defense" against savage forces waiting for liberation in the unconscious; and he asks us to regard the "incredible savagery" going on in our civilized world as the inevitable consequence of leaving man to "digest his sins alone when he is not too sure of divine grace." Left to the resources of his own moral conscience, the sting of a bad conscience will spur man to "cross the threshold of the unconscious mind and become aware of those impersonal forces that make him the unconscious instrument of the wholesale murderer in man."

It is true that Jung did not hold the scientific mind and Protestantism directly responsible for what he called "savagery," but what is more insidious, he called for the "protection of the ecclesiastical walls carefully erected and reinforced since Roman days" to keep the dark forces of the unconscious at bay. He disposed of the phylogenetic sociality of nature by treating it as a primordial lycanthropic monster, and he was most careful to distinguish between this level of the unconscious and the psychogenetic inheritance of archaic Christian symbolism. We are in fact warned that our only defense against the "monster" is to reinforce the preconscious "theological archetypes." In contrast with Jung's concept of the "impersonal beast" in man, quite a different view of the instinctual mind is taken by Erik Erikson: "Our habitual relationship to what we call beasts in nature or 'instinctual beastliness' in ourselves may be highly distorted by thousands of years of superstition, and there may well be resources for peace in our animal nature if we only learn to use it...."[15] Evidence from Jung's dream analyses for the inheritance of archaic emotions in the preconscious is not in dispute; it is his interpretation of the historical function of these "sacred archetypes" that I reject and also the implication that these visions and images of "archetypal dogma" are (besides being innate) uninspired and uninfluenced by the religious taboos and conditioning of a society that is itself pathological.

Jung did not have the concepts of physical anthropology and ethology to guide him and rescue him from his confusions, and he was deaf to the historical dialectic of Hegel, Marx, and Sartre. He was therefore able to perform the hat trick of A: equating the conscious level of the mind with science, B: the preconscious with Christian dogma, C: the unconscious of nature with a primordial Devil. For Jung there are three "creeds," representing three levels of the mind: science, religion, savagery. The historical philosopher and the physical anthropologist who join hands at the frontiers of prehistory and history do not come into the picture at all:

As a doctor I might of course adhere to the "scientific creed" . . . but I cannot tell my patients what I myself do not fully believe . . . a scientific theory is soon superseded by another. . . . The suffering God-Man may be at least five thousand years old . . . the Protestant has lost the sacred images which have been a safe way of dealing with the *unaccountable* [my italics] forces of the unconscious mind. . . . The Catholic "directors of conscience" have often more psychological skill and insight.[16]

The crux of the issue is that Jung does not recognize or respect a self-determined ethical "I," and when he does toy with the concept he confuses its qualitative significance with the abstraction "the sum total of human personality":

There is only one condition under which you might legitimately call the inner voice your own, namely, when you assume your conscious personality to be a part of a whole or to be a smaller circle contained in a bigger one . . . but so far as the sum total of human personality is concerned one has to admit the impossibility of a complete description or definition.[17]

Since Jung did not like dialectic philosophy he was forced to leave the problem of the split psyche and the elusive "ethical I" unresolved. If empirical science could not produce a satisfactory and permanent image of man's destiny and responsibility, then the intelligent patient, like Jung himself, must sedate and sterilize the "phylogenetic savage" with the dogma of religious faith. Beauty must tame the Beast. In other words, the patient's conscience must be surrendered to the "catholic directors of conscience." The real problem, however, is to bring the patient face to face with a natural ethos that is impervious to the sacred archetypes of establishment psychiatry, especially when one considers that those archetypes are tailor-made for the corrupted morality of a society motivated by destructive competition and greed.

Jung's therapeutic advice may well help to cure a fashionable neurosis, but it also helps to perpetuate a race of mindless "little brothers" who can be relied upon to do what they are told. Psychiatric treatment in this context is the death of the soul.

CHAPTER 11

The Great Amoralist

Charles Dickens has shown, if in shame we need him to remind us, that human kindness and the joy of living can flourish in an environment that is poverty-stricken. In the most dire circumstances a spirit of goodwill may prevail so that no bad can come out of it. It would seem therefore that what is commonly called a "bad character" can be inborn and that the failure to develop a sense of social responsibility and duty to others may be the result of a genetic defect in the emotive physiology of the individual, regardless of whether the environment is materially affluent or impoverished. Arthur Guirdham writes:

It may be that strong illicit urges, severely repressed in previous generations, induced flaws in the endocrine-autonomic chain, resulting in the eruption of organic or functional symptoms in subsequent generations. . . . It seems to me that the symptoms in the more bizarre forms of schizophrenia are best explained by postulating the existence of pre-personalities in the patient afflicted.[1]

An example of psychopathic degeneracy in which factors of both a defective genetic constitution and a pathological environment combine appears in almost a classic form in the Plymouth Brethren family that produced the psychopathic killer John George Haigh:

Haigh was brought up in the literalist fundamentalism of Plymouth Brethren parents in a fanatically religious atmosphere, where newspaper reading and listening to the radio were forbidden, where the wrath and vengeance of God was held over his head as punishment for every trifling misdemeanour, and where the belief in salvation through the drinking of blood of the sacrificed lamb of God was impressed upon him in the gruesome literal sense in which an African witch doctor would understand this mystic ritual.[2]

It would be quite wrong to explain Haigh's behavior as simply the product of a puritanical environment and equally wrong to attribute the moral degeneracy of his fanatical parents to their upbringing and environment. Somewhere a genetic defect was already at work. Haigh was in fact diagnosed as a paranoid schizophrenic with traces of mongolism.

Unless we accept the case for inborn characters both good and bad, we shall have to explain the innate talent and potential of Johann Christian Bach (the son of Johann Sebastian) as the product of a musical habitat and the tutelage of his father. Into this hybrid concept we would also have to bring the statistics of the Bach family, which was musically productive for seven generations, and the fact that of more than sixty Bachs known by name all but seven were organists and musicians of a high order.

The theory that children are no more than what they are made to be by the disciplines of an inherited culture assumes that they are born amoral and asocial by nature. We are often told stories about abandoned children who were fostered by wolves and bears and who grew up to be "amoral" and savage, but in an earlier chapter we saw how the pet or zoo monkey that has been isolated from a natural way of life (for which it is phylogenetically prepared in the womb) also grows up to be a desocialized idiot. Similarly, the natural instincts of children cannot develop and reach maturity outside their own society. For this reason the fantasy *Lord of the Flies* (which concentrates on the sadistic behavior of children marooned on an island) is valuable only as a confirmation of the point I am making: had the "innately sadistic" children been left with a tribe of Jivaro Indians in the Amazon jungles, they would either have integrated naturally on the basis of a Jivaro culture or they would have suffered the consequences of a highly ethicopolitical and ritualized act by the Jivaros; i.e., they would have been eaten.

On an adult level a hostile environment may contain elements that are good for the temperament of those who thrive on adversity. It may force the good to do evil, but it cannot force the good to want to do evil. The most sophisticated techniques in brainwashing can only substitute for the existing psyche another that acts as an autonomous slave to a new master. It may be argued that such is the power of the external that the character of an individual can be shaped by it willy-nilly: that if the body is mutilated, the will broken, and the mind reduced to an automaton, then the fundamental character will have been changed. All this means is that the emotive will of a moral conscience can be destroyed, so that the individual that was is no longer there to be judged, praised, or condemned. In short, an environment can destroy a man or it can be favorable for the development of his character, but it cannot make him what he is not. The success with which he copes with stress will be fundamentally fixed by his innate character. The more he understands himself and therefore his own limitations, the more successful he will be in developing his natural potential. A tone-deaf individual may well develop his character by struggling with the problem of learning music, and he may achieve a degree of success that satisfies him, but if he sets himself the goal of creating on the level of a great composer he is a fool.

No action or decision by a hostile external can ever be compulsory in relation to the free will. Suppose a most powerful despot were to order a group of men to bring their sons for sacrifice to a god whom they do not believe in. The men are spiritually free to rebel and put the despot to death; they may bow to the will of the despot to save their own lives or they may consign their sons to death with the expectation of a successful rebellion in the future. Whatever they do they will have suffered, but they will not have suffered the compulsion of an external will. They will have willed to save their own lives by sacrificing their sons, or willed to save their sons by fighting and if necessary dying for them, or willed to sacrifice some of their sons to gain time for a future victory. The fundamental "compulsion" is their own free will. This free will is not an absolute or metaphysical entity. It is, of course, conditionally free, but only to the extent that it depends upon the challenge of pain and adversity for the development and stability of its own life and character.

The view that the fundamental character of a man can be fixed by environment also leads to the theory that all criminal behavior can be "cured" by education and rehabilitation, a theory which implies that the offenders in some strange and mysterious way are all fundamentally moral. I am not denying the importance of social reform, nor am I concerned only with the error of attributing the "evil" in man to environmental stress. My intention is to try to show that the operator of that force we call evil will never be understood until our traditional concepts of the moral, the immoral, and the amoral are re-examined in a new context.

Although the physiology of the brain will not give us a moral criterion for the emotional behavior of man, it is important to consider some of the fundamentals of brain anatomy in relation to its evolution, if only to reach the frontiers of research where neurophysiology ends and psychology begins.

The neurophysiologist Dr. Paul MacLean names three basic divisions of the cortex: archicortex, mesocortex, and neocortex. These correspond with the reptilian, lower mammalian, and higher mammalian brain. In the course of evolution the older areas have formed a limbic system that is tied close to the brain stem. This limbic or closed-in primitive cortex has been surrounded by a rapid growth of the neocortex. As such, the neocortex is a new superimposed superstructure that has no direct and automatic control over the older brain. MacLean writes:

Considered in the light of Freudian psychology the old brain would have many of the attributes of the unconscious Id. One might argue that the visceral brain is not at all unconscious (possibly not even in sleep) but rather eludes the grasp of the intellect because its animalistic and primitive structure makes it impossible to communicate in verbal terms.[3]

Research in brain pathology has shown that the limbic cortex, or older brain, is able to derange the functions of the neocortex. This can lead to a variety of pathological conditions, including rabies and epilepsy. Patients with limbic epilepsy sometimes show all the symptoms of schizophrenia. The dichotomy of this function has been called a "schizophysiology of the limbic and neocortical systems in the brain." Experiments on monkeys have shown that the stimulation of certain areas in the limbic system will produce penile ejaculation, salivation, aggression displays, and many other reactions. There are many intermediary levels between the limbic system and the neocortex that interact continuously and in a manner which research has been unable to explain.

It is well known that sexual maturation from the infant to the adult reproduces the evolution of the brain in its transition from the older mind to the new. Arthur Koestler, however, makes the strange comment that this maturation is inevitably pathological and can never be "complete" even in the normal person because "the schizophysiology is built into our species." In this way Koestler attributes all the madness and brutality in human history to an "evolutionary mistake in brain-building." This kind of closed-system thinking seems bent on resolving the positive and negative elements in the psychodynamics of the human mind (which must inevitably experience some pain and frustration in order to be a mind!) into a mysterious entity which Koestler calls a "dynamic balance." To achieve this sublime state Koestler looks hopefully to the discovery of a magic pill or a new technique in brain surgery that will close the gap between the conscious and the instinctual mind. To my mind, the concept of a "dynamic balance" conveys no more than a "balanced dynamic," and it sounds very much like a dynamic draw in a match between the Buddhist Monk Rangers and Swiss Yodelers United. Whatever the solution to the human dilemma, a "dynamic equilibrium" of emotive forces is clearly the fantasy of a closed mind, a piece of utopian logic which asks us to contemplate a victorious stability that has no instability to stabilize.

Unless we take the human psyche as a unity that depends on a conflict with itself, we shall never understand how a conflict may lead to a neurosis in one individual and to intuitive and creative behavior in another. It is, of course, important to understand the generating mechanisms in the interaction of the old brain with the new, but this education can never provide us with a criterion for understanding the polarity of sickness and health in terms of moral self-determination. The "I" cannot know the "I" in terms of its psychomotor physiology (nor indeed of its "psychology") when the phylogenetic resources of its imagery and intuitions are taken in the Freudian context of "the self-assertive ego of animalism."

The same confusion persists in speculative theory on the neurophysiological aspects of man's self-transcending emotions. Specialists have distinguished two main forms of emotion in the nervous system: the sympathetic and the parasympathetic. The general view is that these opposing elements are mutually antagonistic, though they may be correlated in some way. Whatever the interaction, it is assumed that the creative emotions are in conflict with the self-assertive demands of the animal mind (which corresponds roughly with the Freudian Id). This is the old mistake of elevating the moral and artistic emotions of man to a transcendentalism for which there is no antecedent or precursor in the older mind. But when we put this abstract dichotomy between "self-transcendentalism" and the "older mind" in the context of living behavior, we do in fact find an analogy for it in the conflict between individual assertiveness and species-preservation, or as I would say between the animal ego and the social ethos of the group. In other words, there is no reason to assume that the limbic cortex is fundamentally and instinctually at war with the "self-transcending neocortex," unless the particular animal ego is itself pathological. Clearly, if we are going to use a concept like "self-transcending emotions," we must distinguish between a pathological and a healthy transcendentalism—the one sick, escapist, and destructive, and the other healthy and creative.

In my view it is very comforting to have a neurophysiological confirmation of the fact that the "neocortical-self" is tied to the autonomous dynamics of the older mind. Consistent with the concept of a biological premorality, I would expect the self-transcending emotions to be in harmony as well as in conflict with the autonomous drives of the older mind. There is no evidence or logic for regarding them as being fundamentally opposed by what is so glibly referred to as the "self-assertive ego of animalism." Indeed, the "limbic ethos" of Jojo in his wild primate colony would seem to be far less escapist and self-assertive than the "asocial ethos" of a transcendental monk in his monastery and far closer to the social idealism of Marx and Jesus. The point is taken up by Erik Erikson:

The original awe of the inner conflicts which motivate man made his ego seem to be a pathetic compromiser between the Id, which had a monopoly on all instinctual fuel of man's "animal nature," and the Super-Ego, which could claim the support of all-knowing priests, all-powerful and all-embracing institutions. . . . Gradually however the study of the human ego, the guardian of individuality, revealed it to be the inner "organ" which makes it possible for man to bind together the two great evolutionary developments, his *inner life* and his *social planning*.[4]

The "inner organ" to which Erikson refers is, of course, a very elusive operator who refuses to be located and defined in empirical terms. When the neurologist stimulates the patient's brain to move or speak in a certain way, the patient will defend his independent ability to initiate his own movements and decisions by saying: "But you have engineered my behavior. I did not act voluntarily." Clearly, the self-determined "I" that makes its own decisions cannot be defined in neurobiological terms simply because it knows itself as both subject and object to itself; i.e., it is a free as well as a conditioned agent. The criterion of such self-knowledge rests in its own freedom to act or not to act. The "operator," therefore, cannot be defined in spacial and temporal terms, because *where* he operates in the brain and *what* he operates with is not *what* he is. In short, there is a philosopher in the brain whose essential nature is impervious to empirical analysis.

We know that man has inherited the nervous system and the older mind of the nonhuman primates and that the phylogenetic motor patterns of the unconscious are autonomous and spontaneous. We also know that the unconscious has a direct influence on the conscious mind: "The cortex is tied so tightly to the function of the basal ganglia that it can never operate without it." It does not follow for me, however, that the neocortex or conscious mind is the controlling agency; it is simply the organ of the intellect and of self-consciousness. I also regard the concept of the psyche (which is usually understood as the "soul" or "spirit") as inadequate for representing the ethical self. For me, the central authority of the individual must spring from his own moral will. As long as he allows himself to be ruled by a moral authority that is external to himself (such as the state or the church), he fails to identify with his own ethical conscience. Hegel writes: "Ethical principles must not lay their claim on man as external laws to be obeyed; they have their justification in his heart, sentiment, conscience and intelligence."[5] The concept of self-identity will also provide us (as the social conscience) with a moral criterion for judging whether a defective individual is immorally sane, immorally insane, morally insane, or amorally sane, whether in fact he is responsible or not for his crimes.

The traditional moralist tells us: If an evildoer understands the impulse that has seized him as evil and does not carry out his evil intent, he becomes an honest man who resists temptation. If, however, he obeys his evil impulse (and murders a child, for example), it is because his understanding has failed and the act is not understood as harmful; it is willed for him because it satisfies one of his wants. This means that if most of a man's life be given to crimes which inflict pain and death upon countless innocents, as long as he occasionally repents he dies ultimately as a man who is qua moral. Such is the traditional case for morality put by Benedetto Croce: "Evil does not exist as a positive fact, except as a judgement of self in the mind of the evil doer, when *ipso facto* it is good. All judgements of acts as evil are metaphorical."[6] In other words, if the "good thought of not murdering" is absent in the mind of the murderer while he is murdering a child, all we can do is to metaphorically disapprove! We already know that in the abstract the potential for evil is all one with the potential for good. But if a given man devotes his entire life to cruelty and corruption in the pursuit of power or satisfaction for self, and then, in one moment of doubt inspired by a fear of the unknown, repents on his deathbed, he will nevertheless go down in my history book as an evil man and not a victim of folly. I leave those who are disposed to the metaphysics of the transmigration or metamorphosis of souls to wrestle with the paradox of two individuals—the one who lived in the cause of evil and the other who died in self-atonement. Hegel writes: "While man pursues aims of his own to the uttermost, while his knowledge and his will seek his own narrow self apart from the universal, that man is evil."[7]

The utilitarians and the hedonists will tell us that all is the pursuit of pleasure, all is utility; we will what we do and we do what we will, regardless of whether we are driven by a sense of duty or by self-indulgence. The same force of will that inspired Richard to murder a rival for the throne drove Joan to the stake because of her religious convictions. Both sought their advantage in different ways. But when we declare these "advantages" or "pleasures" to be the expression of one quality arising from one and the same impulse, we make an identity out of words, not deeds. The difference in quality persists: the distinction between actions driven by satisfaction for self only and those that reach beyond the self, between self-love and love of family or country, between acts that are moral and those that are useful and economic—whether they bring pleasure or pain. To argue that morality is but another form of self-gratification is to reduce life to a game of words, a disposition much favored by those who do not wish to distinguish the things that have a price from those that have none.

We have considered the negative-will as a potential for evil, but we have not yet defined the distinct character of evil itself. To come closer to the face of evil we must define an "immorality" that by its own logic and sanity cancels out morality altogether, and to do this I believe we must reconstruct our whole conception of the amoral.

The immoral man who is conscience-stricken with guilt is fundamentally and naturally moral. As a moral man he has behaved immorally, but he cannot be absolutely immoral because he remains qua moral. To become by "nature" qua immoral he would have to be nonmoral or amoral. The amoral man who is never conscience-stricken and who feels no remorse is "conscientiously" opposed to morality. In him the immoral has become his emotive will. Unlike the curate's egg that was bad only in parts, the amoral man is an unqualified nonspiritual bad egg. In the eyes of morality he appears as fundamentally immoral, but by his own innate unnaturalness he is incapable of acting with moral intent and is therefore amoral.

To be amoral does not mean that the individual has lost his sanity; indeed it is quite wrong to presuppose that a man is a pathological subject simply because he is amoral. I contend that amorality has reality (as a fact and not a metaphor) only in the context of adult sanity, where its unqualified nonmorality can be clearly recognized in what we call evil. The sanity of amorality is clear to see in Hitler's program for the education of the Hitler Youth: "There must be no tenderness or weakness in the eyes of youth ... they must show the gleam of pride and the independence of the beast of prey .... To eradicate the thousands of years of human culture youth must be pitiless and indifferent to pain."[8]

It is easy to see how the development of an immoral or bad character can be attributed to a bad environment. Nobody questions the evils of a sick environment and its power to destroy the character of a man. We tend, however, to overlook that all environments involve stress of one kind or another. A life without stress is inconceivable. We must therefore explain why one individual will act constructively in coping with the natural stresses and disciplines of life while another rebels, not because of any political or spiritual convictions he may have, but simply because he wills to follow the ambitions of self-interest. For this reason I contend that the dominance or malignant ascendancy of the negative element in the emotive will can be set in motion by an unbridled self-assertiveness that knows nothing of the rights of others. It is in fact only by taking the pathology of the negative will as a self-determined subject that we are able to explain why one man's shame can be another man's "victory."

Should the immoral adolescent persist in satisfying his self-seeking desires regardless of the harmful effects on others, he must sooner or later make his way into immoral society, where his future as a lackey or a master in the profession of crime will be determined by the power of his defective will. For as long as he retains a sense of shame he is qua moral, but the more immorally he behaves the more demoralized he becomes, and should the negative will succeed in ruling the psyche he will retain his sanity only at the cost of losing his moral sense and becoming amoral. Alternatively, he loses his identity and degenerates into a psychotic. That is why those who cannot withstand the stresses of indecision that threaten their moral faith often prefer to take their own lives rather than escape into madness or submit to evil by injuring others.

To be moral we must recognize the immoral as our own negative will, the negative of positive judgment by which our morality is understood. Morality, however, never penetrates the amoral mind. The amoralist is obliged to exile morality and with it the criterion of judgment that depends equally upon the immoral. He does not therefore experience the conflict of the moral conscience. The real threat to his security is not morality but society. Morality does not invade the amoral mind as morality, but as the sociality of morality. In other words, amorality needs the sensuous and intellectual society of its Other, but only for itself. The amoralist is therefore incapable of spiritual love (which would be better described as natural love). He craves excitement and involvement with others, and he dreads the boredom and the isolation he will suffer if deprived of their society. That is why the amoralist is never a recluse. He hates the morality in the very society he craves and must feed on, yet his own security depends on the ability to be a parasite on it and to convert others to his own "faith." To achieve this he must act the various roles attributed to virtue while concealing his amorality. I believe this to be the true character of what we call evil. It is also my conviction that whereas a demoralized depressive or psychopath may be cured, a truly evil and biologically healthy amoralist is incurable.

Endowed with all the resources of a power-crazed emotive will and a supreme pride in using it, the great amoralist may reach the stature of the Moroccan Sultan Ismael Hafid, Leopold II, or Hitler. He does not necessarily have to be pathological or insane. He is more likely to be successful while he keeps his biological health and his sanity, which many of Hitler's underlings who have survived and are enjoying an affluent life know only too well.

The amoralist must in fact remain sane in his own territory, where he invents an ideology so superficially plausible and consistent that it becomes extremely difficult to separate his fantasies from common sense. His genius consists in his ability to infect others with his solipsism while remaining immune himself to moral influence and persuasion of any kind. In this way he makes his fantasies into a reality. These symptoms are apparent in the paranoidal systems of the Ku Klux Klan, apartheid, and other forms of racism. It is easy to see how the hypnotic effects of the pathogenic "inner voice" can pervert and exploit the inborn structure of infant responsiveness in crowd behavior. The point is well made by Dr. L. S. Penrose:

The hypnotized subject reacts unconsciously as though he were a helpless infant biologically dependent upon an infallible parent. . . . It is relevant to observe that soldiers are more easily hypnotized than civilians. The suggestibility of the private soldier is especially enhanced by military training directed towards the perfection of collective activity. For this purpose either the appeal to a sense of perfect security (sleep induction) or the mobilizing of a primitive fear of the unknown (shock induction) is found to be effective. Similar methods of inducing receptivity are not only used by charlatans, like fortune tellers and purveyors of remedies for commercial purposes, they have become an integral part of the technique for the preparation of masses of people for revolution and war.[9]

We see the great danger of oversimplification in the common generalization that Hitler was simply one psychopath among many anonymous violent people whose rise to power concurred with group support. First, unqualified violence is simply the force of aggression raised to its highest power (see chapter 4). In an ethological context men of goodwill are not less or more aggressive than men of bad will. Second, amoral behavior is not necessarily pathological. Third, a great amoralist like Hitler cannot be put into the same category as a depressive who is demoralized and sick and turns his destructive tendencies against himself.

I believe that my reconstruction of the concept of amorality breaks down the metaphysic of the "unqualified" great man. Regardless of his historical impact, it is no longer a question of whether this bogus "genius" is good or sinful, *because only good men are capable of sin.* We can distinguish, for example, between the Napoleon who in his own conscience failed as well as succeeded and the Hitler who is denied moral judgment by both society and himself. He neither earned, deserved, nor wanted the negative salvation of being immoral. Such is the picture that has been given us by those who knew him intimately and well.

Art extolls the great immoralist in drama and prose. He draws his strength from the same instinctual forces that move us all, but if he fails, he fails in his own conscience as well as in history. No such homage attends the fate of the great amoralist. The amoralist can be comic, but he can never be tragic or tragicomic. The essential element in the psychodynamics of Hitler was his amoral sanity and the strength of an emotive will which enabled him to dominate and identify with amoral political forces in the West that were only too willing to support his rise to power. He was a compelling, hypnotic, and highly intelligent orchestrator of evil. Although his crimes will go down in history as one of the greatest tragedies for the human race, he himself was not a tragic figure, and if for a fleeting moment one can disregard the sheer horror of his reality, all that remains is a humorless and comic figure of untragic absurdity. Chaplin understood this well in his film *The Great Dictator.*

CHAPTER 12

Monogamy and Evolution

The evidence I have considered in the earlier chapters would suggest that a historical construction of the psychosocial evolution of the hominid lines is no longer a matter of pure speculation. Much of the new knowledge we now possess, particularly from ethology and physical anthropology, has developed rather than refuted the main hypotheses in the work of the pioneer anthropologist Lewis H. Morgan. An official opposition, however, to his general theory continues. This opposition is part of a general criticism of the social theory of Marx and Engels, who were the main interpreters of Morgan's work. Before I reexamine Morgan's concept of a group-mating system in prehistory, a concept that is important for the present chapter, I must first consider what Marx and Engels really did say on the subject of prehistory and human evolution. The hoary criticism that Marx's historical theory is based on "economic determinism" is answered by Lévi-Strauss:

. . . as we noted, this was not the opinion of Marx and Engels. According to their view, in the pre-capitalist societies kinship ties played a more important role than class relations. I do not believe I am being unfaithful to their teachings by trying, seventy years after Lewis H. Morgan, whom they admired so greatly, to resume Morgan's endeavour—that is, to work out a new typology of kinship systems in the light of knowledge acquired in the field since then, by myself and others. . . . Lewis Morgan's genius at one and the same time founded social anthropology and kinship studies and brought to the fore the basic reasons for attaching such importance to the latter: permanency, systematic character, continuity of changes.[1]

Those who are unfamiliar with the text of Marxist thought and have accepted secondhand interpretations that have described Marxism as "economic determinism" will be enlightened by the following:

The determining factor in History is the production and reproduction of immediate life, but this itself is of a twofold character. On the one hand the production of the means of subsistence, of food, clothing and shelter and the tools requisite therefore; on the other, the production of human beings themselves, the propagation of the species. The social organizations under which men of a definite country live are conditioned by both kinds of production: by the stage of development of labour on the one hand, and of the family on the other.[2]

Stressing the same point in a letter to Kautsky, Engels writes:

It is not barbarism that establishes the primitive character of a society, but rather the degree of integrity of the old blood ties in the tribe. It is these blood ties which must be demonstrated in each particular instance, before drawing conclusions for this and that tribe from isolated phenomena.[3]

Engels's understanding of the historical significance of comparative kinship systems is emphasized by Lévi-Strauss:

It remained for Marcel Mauss to justify and develop Engels's hypothesis that there is a striking parallelism between certain Germanic and Celtic institutions and those of societies having the potlatch (tribal ceremonials concerned with property, rank and inheritance). He did this with no concern about uncovering the specific conditions of a mode of production, which, Engels had already understood, would be useless. But then Marx and Engels knew incomparably more anthropology almost a hundred years ago than Revel knows today.[4]

What, then, are the main objections by so many of our contemporary social anthropologists to the hypotheses of Morgan and Engels? Morgan believed that matriarchal systems of group mating in prehistory preceded the rise of patriarchal society and of the monogamous relationship, a conclusion based on his own field studies among the North American Indians. He was undoubtedly guilty of overinterpretation, but his main object was to demonstrate a relation between kinship and historical continuity, to show that the social evolution of tribal societies presupposes a historical period in which group mating prevailed. Engels himself was well aware that human evolution is an aggregate of heterogeneous societies, each with its own way of life and its own history. His much abused concept of "promiscuous group mating" was not supposed to be taken as an ideological prototype for the individual histories of all prehistoric systems during a historical period of group mating, but to represent a transitional stage during which group mating in general must have preceded the institution of patriarchal monogamy. Attempts have been made to read all manner of queer notions into what Marx, Engels, and Morgan meant by "group promiscuity," but here is what Engels did say:

[referring to prehistoric forms of the human family] . . . we arrive at a form of sexual intercourse which can only be described as promiscuous *in so far as the restrictions later established by custom did not yet exist.* It by no means follows from this that a higgledy-piggledy promiscuity was in daily practice. Separate pairings for a limited time are by no means excluded; in fact, *even in group-marriage they constitute the majority of cases.* And if Westermarck, the latest to deny this original state, defines as marriage every case where the two sexes remain mated until the birth of offspring, then it may be said that this kind of marriage would occur under the conditions of promiscuous intercourse, without in any way contradicting promiscuity, that is, the absence of barriers to sexual intercourse later set up by custom. Westermarck starts with the view that "promiscuity involves a suppression of individual inclinations," so that "prostitution is its most genuine form." To me it seems that all understanding of primitive conditions remains impossible so long as we regard them through brothel spectacles.[5]

Pressing the same point in a letter to Engels in 1882, Marx referred to the ignorance of primeval times shown by Wagner in the text of the Nibelung: "Whoever heard of a brother embracing his sister as his bride?" Marx wrote: *"In primeval times the sister was the wife, and that was moral."*

Most misrepresentations of the historical concepts of Marx and Engels are the result of failing to distinguish between historical and empirical concepts and of misunderstanding the relation between concept and reality. Engels writes:

Are the concepts that prevail in natural science fictions because they by no means coincide with reality? From the moment we accept the theory of evolution all our concepts of organic life correspond only approximately to reality, otherwise there could be no change. On the day that concept and reality absolutely coincide in the organic world, development is at an end. . . . Did feudalism ever correspond to its concept? Founded in the kingdom of the West Franks, further developed in Normandy, in England and Southern Italy, it came nearest to its concept in the one-day kingdom of Jerusalem, which in the Assises de Jerusalem left behind it a most classic expression of feudal order. Was this order a fiction because it achieved a short-lived existence in full classic form in Palestine, and even that mostly on paper?[6]

Clearly the central thought of Marx, Engels, and Morgan on the whole question of social evolution may be summarized as follows: (*a*) there are continuous and discontinuous evolutionary lines from anthropoid submen to *Homo sapiens;* (*b*) there is a historical development from the group-mating systems of early man to the patriarchal and monogamous systems of later civilizations; (*c*) the correspondence of the concept to reality does not mean that every species and society of early man must reproduce a "classic form" of group mating in its own history. These three main points should be kept in mind while we compare the conclusions of Marx, Engels, and Morgan with what we know today.

Engels was accused by the anthropologist Westermarck of drawing false parallels between the family systems of apes and men. Here is Engels's reply to this criticism:

We know next to nothing about the family and other social groupings of the anthropoid apes. The reports contradict one another.

We must therefore for the present reject every conclusion drawn from unreliable reports. . . . Mutual tolerance among the adult males however must have been the first condition for the building of enduring groups before the transition from ape to man could be achieved.[7]

Engels did not know what we know today—that a sample of the mating systems of the ape, baboon, and monkey does in fact support his concept of nonmonogamous mating among wild primates. Had he known what we now know from ethological field studies—that group mating and "mutual tolerance among the adult males" is in fact a necessary condition for the health and stability of all primate societies (with the single exception of pairing in gibbon families)—he could have easily silenced critics like Westermarck who argued that the anthropoid apes were monogamous. The truly astonishing thing is Engels's *intuitive* conviction that mutual tolerance among adult males must be the first condition for "building enduring groups." More astonishing is the fact that many of our contemporary zoologists and physical anthropologists are still peddling a form of Westermarckism. By continuing to describe the mating system of the gorilla as "a harem of females guarded by a jealous overlord," they ignore a vast body of new knowledge from field studies that proves this idea to be quite false and they fail to grasp what Engels understood nearly 100 years ago—that mutual tolerance among the adult males is essential for group solidarity.

In his field study of the mountain gorilla George Schaller describes an encounter between two males—an adult named Outsider, who moved on the periphery of the group, and the leader:

On 23rd September I witness another copulation. The animals were scattered over the slope, resting and absorbing the warm rays of the sun. Outsider stood on all fours, scanning the valley below, when a female appeared out of the undergrowth behind him. She clasped him around the waist and thrust herself against him about twenty times. At first he appeared oblivious but then he swivelled around, grabbed the female by the waist, pulled her into his lap, and began to thrust. The leader, who was lying fifteen feet away, rose and slowly approached the pair. The Outsider desisted and retreated ten feet up hill, but when the leader ambled away after about one minute, the Outsider returned to her . . . . With the female in his lap he thrust rapidly. . . .[8]

Schaller summarizes his observations of gorilla mating behavior as follows:

Females become sexually receptive for three to four days during time of ovulation, which occurs once a month. At such times they appear to initiate sexual contact with a silver backed male of their own choice, and this male need not be the leader and dominant animal in the group. . . . The magnanimity with which the leader shared his females with other males helped to promote peace in the group. . . . Eskimos and other native peoples also found that it caused less dissension to share their wives with visitors than to have them taken by force.[9]

In the reproductive season of the South American Saimiri monkeys the males become more passive and lose the characteristics of masculine aggression, not only in behavior, but physiologically. During this period they become rejected neuters, and the maternal group dominates the social activity of the colony.[10] Female baboons are more aggressive when in estrus, during which time they mate with juvenile and subdominant males and not only the dominant males. Female chimpanzees during estrus are also frequently dominant over the males and other females. A female order of rank in the species *Macaca fuscata* was observed in the Koshima Island field study. This order was based on kinship and social status. The infants of high-ranking females "inherited" or enjoyed the privileges of a higher position in the group compared with infants of lower-ranking females. The leaders in the troop by no means monopolize the females, though they have first choice over the peripheral males. Copulation between mother and son is rarely seen, from which it seems possible that the incest taboo originated earlier than in human cultures. Carpenter's long and detailed study of gibbon populations in northern Siam has shown that the sexes are equal in social status and that either can be seen leading the family group.[11]

There is no sexual dominance in our lagothrix colony. The behavior of the female is positive in its own right in that the male does not (nor could he) insist on copulating without her willingness to do so. Since the rules of dominance require all males eventually to have dominance over the females, support in general must favor the juvenile and adolescent males should they become involved in disputes with high-ranking females. Without male solidarity a dominance hierarchy could never be formed; without a dominance hierarchy, the maximum strength and efficiency within the group for defending territory and protecting the young could not develop. All dominant males act as father-protectors, displaying affection and concern for the young and assuming responsibility for their welfare. Although accents in mating relations shift and change according to the feelings of individual monkeys, sexual activity on the whole is predominantly communal. The following extract is taken from my book on the sexual behavior of the lagothrix colony:

The first woolly monkeys in the colony to mate were Lulu and Jojo. Mating began in January 1965, and continued until October of that year, seven months before the birth of Lulu's baby in April 1966. Jessy reached puberty at five years of age in November 1965. Django, an adolescent male, was by this time more sexually advanced, and he was the first to show an interest in her. Jojo became interested in Jessy during her second oestrus period, when he allowed Django one day's grace and then took over completely for the two days of the oestrus peak. Until Jessy conceived in April 1966, this arrangement between Jojo and Django was repeated at every oestrus period: Jojo taking Jessy during the oestrus peak, and Django for the days immediately before and after the peak. There was no mating and no sexual overtures from Jessy outside the complete four-day period of oestrus. Suby reached puberty at the age of four, and has had five oestrus periods up to the present time. Her overtures were made to a sub-adult Jimmy, who was the first to mate with her. Jimmy offered no serious objections when Jojo subsequently took Suby during the peak periods, and the arrangement was similar to the one with Django and Jessy. Jojo, as always, lost interest after the two-day period, and although Suby continued to make the overtures to him, it was Jimmy who obliged. Suby preferred Jojo, but was always ready to accept Jimmy when Jojo was not forthcoming. At the peak of her second oestrus both Jojo and Django were vying for her, and Jimmy withdrew temporarily from the competitive scene. The relationship between Jojo and Django at this time developed in a strange way: Django was allowed a few hours with Suby during the oestrus peak, and then Jojo would take over. This was precisely the situation in which I expected the two strongest males to become involved in a serious fight, but I was quite wrong. Instead, Django eventually gave way, though not without some resistance and attempts to intercept.[12]

From Carpenter's field study of the Howler (Alouatta) colonies we know there is very little intraspecific fighting among the males, and the estrus females are almost entirely free from sexual jealousy. Mating overtures are performed by both sexes, and disputes among males are extremely rare.[13] Field studies by Goodall and Kortlandt show that chimpanzee groups in the wild are a complex of polygamous and polygynous mating, living in family groups of six to twelve animals. Jane Goodall writes: "Relationships between mature and adolescent males are particularly harmonious. They do not fight over the females. I once saw seven males in succession mate with a single female, with no sign of jealousy or antagonism."

It is clear from the evidence we have considered that the forms of social organization among the nonhuman primates are similar and that the high-ranking males have first choice with the females during estrus. What is so often overlooked in the search for basic systems and patterns (whether in terms of social, sexual, or mating norms) is that all groups of animals in all species are basically survival units. This simple truth not only comes to terms with ecological influences that give rise to a diversity of social systems within the species as well as conspecies, but relates the mating systems to variations in maturation, food supply, territory, breeding, and population controls. In this context a certain amount of random mating meets the problem of excessive inbreeding and reduces the tension of intraspecific competition. There is in fact very little intraspecific aggression in the wild primate groups. When it does occur it is related to ranking disputes and not sex fighting. The play-fights and mock battles that occur in our lagothrix colony are indispensable for maintaining a healthy ranking system in a natural dominance hierarchy. Every aspect of the opponent is explored in these contests, and in this way the most responsible males establish their priority (not ownership) in mating with the females during the estrus peak, when the females are most likely to conceive. Mating, therefore, is subservient to the interests of group solidarity. Dominant males are always alert to danger, protective toward mothers with young infants, social and affectionate with all members of the group, and generally concerned as to their whereabouts and their safety. All these social activities take priority over mating. Even at the estrus peak, when the males are highly excited, mating can easily be distracted. During copulation there are often pauses, when the males stop thrusting and peer around "on guard" for the possibility of danger from outside the group.

There is no evidence in any field of research to support the view that pairing as such is the mark of a peaceful disposition. The evidence points the other way. Carpenter has shown that gibbons, the only wild primates to pair, are so aggressive and hostile to one another that they live in widely dispersed groups. Social organization in the gibbon family group is in fact less developed than any found among other primate species. As a strict tree-dweller and an expert swinger and brachiator, the gibbon has little to fear from predators. Compared with the ground-living baboons, he is less dependent on support from other members of the group. Conversely, baboon society has a complex ranking order based on a dominance hierarchy. Unisexual groups of subadults, females with young, and an elect circle of dominant males live and move in an intricate pattern of social relations based on mutual aid. Being a terrestrial animal, the baboon is constantly on guard for predators and must therefore travel and live collectively. For ground-living primates a highly organized social life based on mutual cooperation and group mating is a condition of survival. Pair bonding would only increase hostility and disperse the collective power of group action.

My point so far has been to stress the fact that neither

monogamy nor polygamy is found in the monkey and ape groups. There are, however, strong ties of friendship, but these are not motivated by the mating drive. The adult males Jojo and Django often greet each other with the emotive cries of "ogh, ogh," lifting their forearms to expose their chests and lying close together while making the emotive sounds of friendship. The adult females Lulu and Elizabeth also greet and "huddle" with each other in this way. The scent and intimacy of close contact with the chest reminds them of their communal interests, since chest rubbing is an essential part of their territory behavior. In all their social activities—play-fighting, appeasement, mating, group feeding, and infant care —these scents strengthen friendship as well as kinship ties. Elements from these activities combine in the erotic satisfaction and feeling of comfort that is derived from hugging and embracing, in an expressive act that signifies a highly individualized and personal feeling of comradeship. I call it love— the love that grows not out of ownership, but from the need for Other.

What *does* emerge from a study of these mating systems is that analogies cannot be drawn to support the theory that monogamy or polygamy was practiced by primitive man. Iris Andreski writes:

If any prehistoric situation of "pair bonding" took place, it was with other members within a larger group, bonded by all the ties of kinship; and that if anything bound an individual male to an unrelated female, the strongest tie might well be that of mutual exploitation. I suspect that in a close-knit group of support, inspiration, comradeship and sexuality, these four factors which are nowadays expected to converge upon the "nuclear" couple, might each be represented by a relationship with a separate individual; only the purely sexual tie being an unrelated partner of the opposite sex, and that possibly the least "bonded."[14]

For a comparative study with existing tribal cultures, the Australian Tiwi tribe represents in many ways the survival of a cultural level comparable with Paleolithic man. The older Tiwi speak of a time when they went naked, built windbreaks for shelter, used clamshells for cutting tools, a flaked stone ax, and lived in family groups each with its own territory for food gathering and hunting. These groups were predominantly polygynous and not monogamous. Eighty-nine systems of these tribes have been listed, including the Tiwi and other Australian aborigines. Seventy-one percent were polygamous, twenty-five percent monogamous, and four percent polyandrous.[15] In the Australian Worora tribe a man becomes the husband of a girl by making a gift to her parents, but her sexual relations are not thereafter limited to him. He lends her to his brothers who could have been husbands in the tribal kinship. No objection is raised should a wife have extramarital sex with another man, provided he belongs to the acknowledged kin.[16]

When we consider the cultural level and mating systems of the Tiwi and other Australian tribes, the evidence suggests that the early hominid primates, such as the *Australopithecenes*, are likely to have lived in a variety of small group-mating systems intermediary between the Tiwi and the ground-living hominoids. The comparative material we have so far considered would seem to support the socioanthropological concepts of Engels and Morgan that the history of a primate genus presupposes a stage of group mating in the hominid lines. There is, however, more evidence to come, particularly with regard to the rise of monogamy in the evolution of matrilineal and patrilineal systems.

CHAPTER 13

The Group Family

The beliefs and emotions of Paleolithic man were centered upon food supply, birth, and death. Archaeological finds and cave paintings in Paleolithic sites show that the central theme in his religion was maternity and the spirit of the life-producing mother. The mother goddess was the central figure of fertility and procreation in the animal world, which extended to the vegetable kingdom where mother earth became the "womb in which the crops were sown."[1]

Discovery of the well-known female figurines known as "Venuses" show that matriarchism prevailed among the late Paleolithic hunters. These figures have been found in Paleolithic settlements in many parts of Europe and Asia:

The "Venuses" are objects and symbols of child-bearing and fertility cults. The face, arms and legs are neglected, while the breasts, belly and thighs are exaggerated to typify the mother. . . . They are inspired by a reverence for women and they served no erotic purpose. In group-marriage the child-bearing mother occupied an important place in the economic and social sphere. . . . The tribal community therefore derived its origin from an ancient ancestress, whom they worshipped.[2]

Mother-goddess clay figurines at Tell Hassuna are seated on circular stools in parturition, and at A'Ubaid and Susa very early types have been recovered modeled with a child held to the breast. Female figurines in the ancient Middle East and the Indus also confirm that early religion was centered on the female significance of procreation: "At Hagia Triada a female of gigantic stature is depicted between two smaller females before a shrine, and everywhere the goddess predominates in Cretan worship; the male when represented at all is always subordinate and later in time than the Great Minoan Mother."[3]

The sculptured Venuses of the Upper Paleolithic express a religion of the mother goddess that extended from Western Europe across to Asia Minor and Siberia. From Neolithic times onward the mother goddess began to lose her position of dominance. In the background there emerged the young male as her son and brother and later as the begetter and personification of the generative force in nature. The function of the boy god was to revive the life of vegetation in the annual cycle of the seasons and of the goddess to give birth to life of which she was the source. As the ritual control of fertility concentrated more on the success of hunting, domestication, and husbandry, the boy god became the sky god who fertilized the earth goddess with rain from heaven. In Greek tradition the marriage of Zeus with goddesses symbolizes the fertilization of the earth by a sacred alliance between heaven and nature. Inevitably a supreme dominant male as the source of creative energy and the god of the sky became the head of the pantheon. In Egyptian text *Re* became the ruler of the Nile valley, and in the oldest Avestan texts we learn that Zarathustra made Ahma Mazda the supreme deity and Father of Reason "who could be known only in thought."[4] With the development of hunting cultures and husbandry the male god usurped the mother goddess as the creative force of generation and eventually became the dominant partner in the sacred marriage. The conception of the father image therefore belongs to the later Neolithic religions of the male sky god and to the monotheism of Judaism, Christianity, and Islam.

According to an old Ibibio legend, there was a time when women outnumbered the men, when only the priestesses knew the secrets of the gods and were thus able to enslave the men. The time came when the men discovered a shrine of the women's cult, containing the masks and fetishes of the power-giving ritual of the Great Mother. Under pressure, the older women revealed the secrets of the sacred ritual, only to be beheaded by the men, who declared that such would be the fate of all women who attempted to participate in the ritual from that day forth. The "fattening ritual" of young virgins is continued today by Ibibio people who have forgotten its origin and sacrificial significance. They regard it as "wholly and solely a women's affair."[5]

In his study of the Trobriand islanders Malinowski has shown that sexual permissiveness is characteristic of matrilineal and not patrilineal systems. The matriarchal clan is certainly not free of exploitation, and in extreme cases it may reduce the status of the young males to one of servitude. Matrilineal systems are nevertheless democratic when compared with the tyranny imposed on women and children by the dominant-male hierarchies of patriarchal systems. Even so, the significance of patriarchal dominance in relation to the evolution of hunting cultures must be recognized in the light of historical necessity. We considered in an earlier chapter how the hunting primate had inherited the stronger physique and innate dominance behavior from the forest hominoids and that the pathogenic conflict between kinship and cruelty brought not only a new sense of loyalty, but a power of envy that inspired the hunting primate to profit by dominating and exploiting others. Leaving aside the corruption of this inherited male dominance, the fact remains that dominant-male hierarchies were necessary for survival as well as for war. In this context war was not a mere accident or by-product of man's nature but a cruel and necessary experience for discovering the virtues of chivalry and peace. Apes cannot go to war, not because they are saints of nature, but because they lack man's ingenuity to do so.

There is little doubt that nomadic hunting groups of early men were contemporaneous with matrilineal agricultural communities and that courage and pride through "the glory of war," as well as the development of new techniques, weapons, and tools, must be held largely to the credit of warlike patriarchal tribes. In these conditions women were inevitably numbered among the spoils of war, leading ultimately to a patriarchal takeover in the agricultural communities. This may well explain why there is less inequality in the social status of women in isolated and peace-loving tribes, such as we find in the Stone Age cultures of the Australian aborigines.

Clearly all the evidence from social anthropology, ethology, and paleontology that we have considered so far throughout this book would seem to contradict the naive theory that the pairing "love bond" is an essential condition for the survival and health of the human family. Iris Andreski writes:

In one major West Coast vernacular, the only word for love is that for mother. By all records, the only important man-woman relationship was that of mother and son. Among Ibibio peasant women who I studied I had the impression that life as an individual began for each only if and when she joined the household of a married son, or sometimes even a son-in-law. That the new African woman should expect love from her husband is still considered to be an impertinence and a highly unwarranted Imperialist innovation.[6]

I noted earlier that the closest approach to the social units of Paleolithic man is seen in the Australian aborigines, who live in small polygynous groups that never reach the extremes of patrilineal societies; nor do they provide any evidence for supposing that the earliest forms of human social organization were based on the nuclear family. This also applies to the Kalahari Bushmen, the Pygmies, and many other hunter-gatherers, all of whom are peace-loving and nonaggressive. The victory of the patriarchal system was the institution of a family hierarchy based on economic dominance by the males: "... on the rule of the man in the family, the procreation of children who could only be his, destined to be the heirs of his wealth—these alone were frankly avowed by the Greeks as the exclusive aims of monogamy."[7]

The chief attribute of the patriarchal family was the organization of a number of persons under a paternal head. For the Romans *familia* signified the number of slaves belonging to one individual and *familia id est patrimonium*, a social group consisting of a paternal head with the power of life and death over his wife, children, and slaves. Patriarchal communities were still in existence at the end of the nineteenth century among the Serbs and Bulgars.[8] In the South Slavic Zadruga, several generations of sons of one father and their wives lived together in one household, tilling their fields in common and clothing themselves from the common store. Kovalevsky writes: "In the Russian patriarchal communities the head of the house strongly abused his position with the younger women, particularly with his daughters-in-law. Often he converted them into a harem, as eloquently expressed in many Russian folk songs."[9]

The original function of monogamy, whether in its early patriarchal forms or the later Athenian family, was certainly not the fruit of individual sex love. It was based not on a natural relationship, but on the victory of private property and male inheritance over the collective ownership of the prehistoric group family. The strict and legal rigidity of monogamy as a "marriage of convenience" throughout its history has in fact made it the enemy of love. The early forms of romantic sex love were echoed not in conjugal love, but in the praises of poets who describe in glowing colors "the knight who lies with his love, the wife of another, while the watchman stands guard outside ready to call him at the first signs of dawn."[10]

It is true, of course, that a creative love is not experienced by trying to sustain a romantic passion. Nor can a mature love develop where marriage is used as an insurance against the fear and anxiety of being alone and unwanted. Mature love is founded upon a creative relationship, one in which both partners find a greater sense of purpose in life and more freedom in each other, more freedom, that is, to develop their individual character and needs. Love, therefore, whatever else, is also a development of character. But in a society of manipulators and manipulated it is exceedingly difficult for such a love to develop and survive. More often than not a narcissistic orientation takes over, so that a natural faith and courage to act on experience and self-responsibility is undermined by jealousy, anxiety, and an obsession for intellectual certainty. People study child psychology instead of children. The intellect becomes a substitute for living. Love is sought in incompatible relationships founded upon erotic passion, economic security, and a pathological fear of emotional isolation.

No one can deny the naturalness of a heterosexual marriage of love based on social equality. But when such a pair bond is reduced to a legalized monogamy based on the economic dominance of the male, the way is clear for a breakdown in the very nature of man. More than a century ago Marx said: "In the pairing-family the group is reduced to its last unit, its two-atom molecule, to one man and one woman."[11] In its modern form the nuclear family has become the basic and most vulnerable consumer unit for the industrial states of East and West to exploit. The more these units are crowded together in blocks of proletarian flats or in the housing estates of suburbia, the more socially isolated they become. A close parallel is found in zoos, which reproduce a pattern similar to monogamous isolation by placing social animals like monkeys and apes in isolated "breeding pairs" side by side in rows of proletarian cages. In these conditions the father gorilla must be frequently separated from the mother and the baby taken away from the mother should she show signs of eating it.

This dialectic of "crowded isolation" suffered by the nuclear family produces its own pathology of frustration and violence in an emotional war between parents and their children, as well as between parents and infants in the growing phenomenon of child bashing. Alternatively, the taboos of "respectability" mutilate the realities of life, so that education in morality and sex becomes a major issue to be handled with kid gloves. As R. D. Laing has said, the function of the conventional family "is to repress Eros: to con children out of play: to brainwash their 'dirty' minds so that they cannot see through our dirty tricks: to induce a fear of failure: to promote a respect for work: to promote a respect for 'respectability.' "[12]

In the tribal family children are observers of all adult activities including birth and nursing, and they share the fullest and most realistic experiences of fear whenever danger threatens the community. As they grow older and more self-sufficient, the mother turns her attention to new babies or resumes old friendships. They, similarly, relinquish their claims to her intimate affections and occupy themselves with the tough business of living.

Mothers in the New Guinea Dani tribe are often seen comforting their children at the breast until they are three years old. In this way the change from nourishment and consolation is continuous with the nurturing of security and independence. With no kind of formal teaching the Dani people transmit their culture to the young by direct contact with the major events of life. By the time children are five years old they already know about death, sex, gardening, house building, and pig keeping (see plate 13). In the game of "village" they outline an entire village, including fences and homes, with arancaria seeds. These models are replicas of what children see when they look down at their compounds from the fields high on the mountainside. In the spear game, groups of players throw toy spears at a hoop of twisted cane as it rolls past them. Children are not patronized and made to feel the limitations of their youth. This has nothing to do with the fact that they mature early. They are well trained in the ceremonies of dance and song, and they are not shy and secretive about their sexual ambitions. Even before weaning they share their demands for attention with their extended family; their age groups will always be available for play and their grandparents for comfort.

The Group Family: Denmark

In many countries, particularly Denmark, the break from isolated pair marriage to nonmonogamous family groups has developed to such an extent that governments are now wrestling with the problems of new legislation regarding taxation, property ownership, and registration of birth. It is difficult to say how many group families there are in Denmark at the moment. Their organization *Kollektive Koordineringen* published in their latest list the names of forty established groups, but consider that there are more than one hundred groups at various stages of development in the country at the moment, with the number growing all the time.

A report on these families in *Bogen Om Storfamiliere* tells us that the most successful groups are those that have either purchased their own houses or taken a long lease. Domestic planned economies seem to function well in some groups and badly in others. Decisions and agreements on domestic issues, policies relating to news media and television reporters, and personal problems concerning sex and the care of children all occupied a great deal of time. One member said that in the family group there were so many exciting and absorbing things to be seen and heard in a single day that one year in the group was comparable with ten years in the conventional family.

With regard to sex, most members thought the greatest problem was their own anxiety about sex and the suppression of sexual activity. More important was the opportunity to experience and accept one's own and other people's ability to love, not to prescribe how everybody should go about their sex life. Most agreed that their own inhibitions were rooted in idealistic notions imposed on them in childhood. In the traditional monogamous family parents are unable to respond when the sexual urges of children are directed toward them. In this way society ensures that the overwhelming part of the population grows up with sexual anxiety and hostile feelings toward sex. This chokes the freedom of self-expression and favors the authoritarian system.

It was realized that the group family has an extremely important part to play in the rearing of children, but the opportunities it offered could be used well or badly. It is a great advantage for children to have several adults to turn to, provided these adults can agree on how the children should be brought up; otherwise the children become suspicious and feel insecure. It is, of course, possible to give children an open and positive attitude to sex in the monogamous family, but the possibilities are hardly as great as in a group family with several children. In the group there is greater scope for erotic play between children of the same age. The natural behavior of children also puts the adults in situations where their own inhibitions are put to the test.

In many of the least successful and less stabilized groups the interviewer could see little more than confusion. There was no general agreement on how children should be brought up or who was to look after them. Members with no children of their own found they had little interest in children. Many were aware of the problem and simply hoped the situation would improve with more experience. There was also conflict and disagreement about forming close friendships outside the group. Some members agreed it was stimulating and healthy to have outside friends visit them, but they opposed the forming of strong external friendships. Meetings and discussions on this problem led to a great deal of confusion and friction. The least radical members were able to veto the decisions of those who believed that a stable group should evolve its own life-style, one that would in itself inhibit the forming of close emotional relationships outside the group. The weakness and instability of the less successful groups seemed to stem from the lack of a common aim and the kind of responsible leadership that sustains a unity of purpose.

A strengthening of the very factors I consider essential for the health of the group family is clear to see in the relative success of the *Kana Collective*, a group of fourteen adults and four children who live in a large farmhouse north of Copenhagen. In contrast with the immature groups, the *Kana* group is marked by its unity of purpose and also by the happiness of its children. All the members had met each other and developed a strong feeling of unity during the student rising in Denmark in the spring of 1968. One member, a social anthropologist named Henrik, said that he had not felt particularly frustrated or unhappy before the group was formed. He believed that a unified group family would be better equipped to withstand the relentless pressures of establishment politics and morality and the sickening impact of advertising.

One of the most positive achievements of the sex life of the *Kana* group was that the men as well as the women had developed the ability to conquer conventional inhibitions and to express openly a great affection for one another. The climate of the family's sex life had also been found very good for the children. One member remembered his own childhood, when there had been a great deal of sexual activity between himself and his friends from the age of six, but always with the fear that one must remain secretive about it and on no account discuss it with grown-ups. The children in the *Kana* family made no secret of their own erotic behavior. Henrik's observations had convinced him that the so-called latent period from the age of seven until adolescence was no more than a myth and most likely the result of repression.

There seemed to be few problems regarding sex roles in terms of domestic responsibility, labor, and privileges. Merete (a psychologist, age twenty-four and mother of Maria, age seven) said that household chores and cooking were shared equally between the sexes, though the women tended to leave work like carpentry to the men. In her view this was due to a traditional upbringing in which the female is trained to be exclusively a female. She referred to many women she knew who were efficient at odd jobs and carpentry. One of the main problems was finding the time for individual study and the opportunity for engaging in outside political work. Demands by the group's internal life had so far made this extremely difficult. They referred to the ease with which the conventional married man, who uses his home as a hotel, can afford to be preoccupied with outside activities. Although the events of group life were more educational and stimulating, there was also the danger of too much emotional involvement. With all the advantages of a shared economy and the convenience of mutual help in practical matters, it remained an enormous undertaking to really know and understand people. Henrik thought that smaller, well-integrated groups of eight to ten adults would avoid the emergence of cliques and reduce the strain of too much personal involvement. Ruth said that communal living had made it very clear that one person cannot satisfy all the needs of another and that there are so many potentials that cannot be realized when they are tied to the monogamous bond. Merete said it was wonderful to always have someone to be with when one felt the need, and yet be able to be alone. She also believed that one had to be a reasonably stable person in the first place to profit by communal living. The group family could not be used as a prop for personal failings. Those who needed constant emotional support should not enter a group family.

On the future of the *Kana* group the members were confident that the group family offered more security and happiness than can ever be found in pair marriage. They were all interested in the possibility of an economic production or industry that would occupy the group as a whole. Some had suggested a market garden, so that all could make a living at home. They also looked to a future in which all groups, small and large, could work together to build a socialist college for revolutionary studies. Merete thought this should come later, that the real revolution was concerned with personal relationships and a better way of educating and caring for children. The general feeling, however, was to withdraw from pretentious talk and great goals in the future when there was so much to be learned and achieved in reorganizing their own life. Summing up, Henrik said: "I think there is a far greater emotional, intellectual, and erotic communication within the group family than you will find anywhere else in society— otherwise they would hardly have much reason to be here."

The experiences of the Danish family communities show clearly that the new freedoms which develop in new relationships also bring their own tensions and problems. This would suggest that those who cannot profit by new experiences may well find traditional relationships more comfortable than unconventional ones. There is no ideal human relationship that will serve as a model for all to follow. Individuals can fail or succeed in their personal relations regardless of any "system" of living together. The group family therefore cannot eliminate the possibility of emotional conflict and changes of heart. But whereas such conflicts and breakdowns in the parent relationship are frequently disastrous for children in the nuclear family, a stable group family offers more protection and security for children as well as for their parents.

Although the roles of father and uncle are socially reversible in the group, it is natural for the biological father to want to act as the real father to his own children, especially when this desire is shared by the mother. All the more so when the pair bond is spiritually and physically strong in its own right. The critic may insist that such a "privilege" reproduces the father fetish of traditional monogamy. This is not necessarily so. The fact is that most fathers will want to play a positive role in the care of infants as well as juveniles, even though the biological role of the mother is fundamental and more consuming. Significant also is the fact that a child develops a desire to know its own father and to find its early security in a close and intimate relationship with that father. Most mothers also welcome help from the father in the labor of comforting and attending to the needs of a growing infant. For these reasons I believe that all forms of new family communities should encourage stable pairing.

Whatever form the parent-child relationship may take, whether in the conventional extended family or in any of the modern group communities, children will interact and identify with father-uncles and mother-aunts regardless. As children grow and their confidence increases, they develop a natural desire for more independence and come to rely less on any exclusive love and attention the biological parents may wish to bestow upon them. The affinities and affections of juveniles are shaped by their own skills and those they work with, increasingly so until they are able to make up their own minds on the question of personal relationships. Such has been my experience and that of colleagues in other groups.

I like to think that Lewis Morgan had the new family communities in mind when, nearly a century ago, he looked to a revival of the ancient gentes, or family clans, of the Iroquois Indians. Morgan wrote: "The dissolution of society bids fair to become the termination of a career on which property is the end and aim, because such a career contains the elements of self-destruction. Brotherhood in society, equality in rights and privileges, foreshadow the next plane of society to which experience, intelligence and knowledge are steadily tending. It will be a revival, in a higher form, of the liberty, equality and fraternity of the ancient gentes."[13]

Hierarchy and Responsibility

We saw that one of the greatest problems for the Danish family groups was decision making on matters of general policy and the dangers of the group becoming too large for personal and intimate relationships to be sustained. Discussions also seemed to lack a chairman, and there were no signs of coming to terms with the problems of leadership. It is understandable that the groups will regard hierarchy and leadership as ideological monsters imported from a decadent culture. What does not seem to be understood is that responsible leadership in a democratic family group is not a power structure hierarchy based on political and economic dominance. Lacking a healthy hierarchic structure, many of the groups show few signs of being stabilized or mature. There seems to be no common aim to hold them together, either in their work or in a political ethic that defines their objectives in relation to society.

For those who confuse authoritarianism with the fundamental need of the human animal for natural restraint, the very concept of hierarchy and leadership is seen as the enemy of individual freedom. A great deal of new knowledge from the field of anthropology confirms the fact that the nature of the human animal is tied to kinship and leadership. The work of Sahlins and others has shown that there is no political and economic exploitation among the Ituri Pygmies, Kalahari Bushmen, Eskimos, and the Australian aborigines. In all these hunter-gatherer cultures counsel is given by elders who avoid prominence and possessions. The acceptance of authority of the Plains Indian chief by his followers is entirely the result of his ability, generosity, and compassion. Leaders in the Melanesian village present the best food to others and leave the remainder for themselves.

The historical importance of this new knowledge is ignored by the French anthropologist Georges Balandier. His conclusions are that all hierarchic systems are based on inequality and domination and that the conflicts arising from this are the main agents of historical development. He warns us that the rejection of hierarchic systems structured on domination and sexual segregation runs counter to a more natural life. Balandier's evidence for these conclusions is taken from precolonial African societies, many of which were (and still are) linked by terrorist societies that maintain a privileged elite and a proletariat of women, children, and slaves. In this way Balandier ignores all the anthropological evidence for the functioning of healthy and responsible hierarchies in existing as well as early societies of man and leaves us instead with the conclusion that the most natural social systems for men are hierarchic structures based on inequality, male domination, age status, and sexual segregation!

Clearly the prevailing confusion on the function of hierarchy is the error of equating despotic hierarchies with healthy hierarchies. Self-healing "therapy communities" remain self-defeated because they have rejected leadership and authority. They could as well try to dispense with organization and discipline. It is true that man by nature is also self-motivated and that he may feel discipline and restraint as an external authority that robs him of his freedom. But without authority and restraint of any kind we would never become socialized, and without self-assertion we could not learn the folly of opposing the ethic of mutual aid and social responsibility.

CHAPTER 14

The Sky God

The traditional moralist will say that the ethic of the new family communities, which practice the political, social, and sexual equality of both men and women, is a corruption of the most natural and fundamental relationship between man and woman and that a divine biology of sexual dimorphism has already decreed that the male shall be dominant and the female passive.

We all know that the "passive ovum" awaits the penetration of the "active spermatozoon," but this does not mean that the most natural forms of sex love between *people* (not "sexual dichotomies") must dance to the hoary tune of "male pursuit and penetration." Many women like to be initiators and take dominant positions in the sexual act. For them the idealized behavior of the "passive female" is unnatural. There are also "superfemale men," who may even win a beauty contest, yet psychologically they are genetic males. Such people do not always fit so easily into the category of transvestites who may or may not desire hormone therapy. Many are unconcerned about their "gender identity" and are quite happy to establish their individuality in their behavior.

When we look for the dynamics of sexual reproduction in the beginning of biological evolution, in the cell life of the Protozoic period, we find that sociality and bisexuality play the dominant part in the reproduction and survival of the most primitive forms of life. The amoebas form communities of slime molds, which are self-reproducing. These communities are formed by mounting groups of amoebas that are attached to a dominant and central mold. The founder core expands and takes on a sluglike shape and then gradually arises into a capped and erect phallus of slime mold. The spore head is then dispersed by contact with passing forms of pond life, thus continuing the cycle of aggregation and reproduction.

It could be argued that the slime-mold "phallus" is both a biological and symbolical precursor of "male dominance" in the Protozoic period, but this does not appear to be so if we follow the evolutionary career of this "dominant element" when it breaks away from the bisexual host to enjoy the privileges of a "dynamic male" in the world of the insect. The role of the female praying mantis in her relationship with the male is hardly submissive. Should she eat his head before coitus, he fulfills his mission with renewed vigor: "The female ate the male's right front leg, decapitated and gnawed into his thorax. The male continued the attempt to obtain entrance to the valvules, and he succeeded as she spread the part open and union took place. The next morning she devoured her spouse completely and nothing but the wings remained."[1] In this way, after the male's one and only act of copulation, the female secures his absolute fidelity for life.

It is legitimate to draw analogies from animal life to illustrate the nature and function of instinctual drives inherited from our animal ancestors, but these analogies can easily become fantasies instead of conclusions based on the facts of animal behavior. Comparative evidence has been used to support the common view that woman is divergent and man convergent, that woman is less aggressive and therefore less creative. Support for this concept of fundamental submissiveness in female psychology is nowhere to be found in early religion and myth. The mother goddess, as we saw in the previous chapter, was the central figure of fertility in Paleolithic religion, and the dominant-mother image still survives in the legends and myths of existing tribal cultures, where she appears as the aggressive mother spirit "in whose womb the crops must be sown." In Egyptian iconography the male sky god and the female mother earth are actually inverted. According to the convincing analysis of Maris Delcourt, the Sphinx represented a female monster who waylaid and raped young men. This inversion of the sky-earth (dominance-submission) relationship is repeated in the "repulsive witch" figure in the mythology of the Hopi Indians. A young hero wandering in the forest is confronted by a dominant mother spirit, who confers on him her power of dominance provided he submits to her advances. The historical reality of the "aggressive priestess" is reenacted by a pathogenic old woman in the fire dance ceremony of the Ituri Pygmies. An old Ibibio legend refers to a time when only the priestesses knew the secrets of the gods and were thus able to enslave the men. It survives today in the Ibibio "fattening ritual of the virgins," the significance of which is regarded by Ibibio men as "solely a women's affair." In another myth of the Hopi Indians the hunter is confronted by a dominant mother figure who lives in the desert as the "Mother of Animals": "He who meets her in her bloody clothes is so frightened that he has an erection, of which she takes advantage to rape him, after which she rewards him with unfailing success in hunting."[2]

It is true, as one writer has said: "Basic biological differences are reinforced in man by the division of labour that makes adult sex roles differ far more in humans than they do in nonhuman primates"; but these "differences" have developed in our society to a point where the role of the suburban housewife has been reduced to one of a mere spectator of life. It may be argued that the political and economic domination of woman is not a unique character of our male-made industrial society, that women suffered even more degradation in the tribal cultures of precolonial Africa. This observation, however, ignores the role of women in the earlier indigenous cultures of the Kalahari Bushmen and the Bambuti Pygmies, who stabilized their internal health by preserving a closer kinship with nature. There is no exploitation of women among the Pygmies of the Ituri Forest. The anthropologist Colin Turnbull writes:

In Bambuti society women have a full and important role to play. There is relatively little specialization according to sex. Even the hunt is a joint effort. A man is not ashamed to pick mushrooms and nuts, or to wash and clean a baby. Women are free to take part in the discussions of men.[3]

In the short time of our permissive society the young female today displays a great deal more natural aggression, spontaneity, and independence than did her mother in the nineteen forties. Nevertheless the argument for "pursuit and penetration" as opposed to female "pursuit and accommodation" continues. We still hear about the alleged superiority of the male in intellectual and creative achievement and that the "creative ability" of women is best confined to child raising and beautifying the home. These false dichotomies between parenthood and citizenship, between biological and social responsibility, between "domestic art" and "great art," take us right back to the days of Otto Weininger's denigration of women in his book *Sex and Character*, published in 1906.

Weininger wrote: "The woman's desire is to play the passive and never the active part in the sexual act . . . her inactive large egg-cells are sought out by the mobile active spermatozoa . . . . Femaleness can never include the genius. When women do something of importance in the scientific world, it is always because of a man in the background whom they desire."[4] These sentiments are echoed almost word for word by the psychiatrist Anthony Storr: "The male spermatozoon swims actively whilst the ovum passively awaits its penetration . . . . It is highly probable that the undoubted superiority of the male sex in intellectual and creative achievement is related to their greater endowment of aggression . . . there have been no women of genius comparable to Michelangelo, Beethoven or Goethe . . . . "[5] Both Weininger and Storr are dedicated victims of sky god ideology. Like Weininger, Storr believes that only men can "reach for the stars" and that the creative ability of women is best left to "the bearing of children and the making of a home."[6] We saw in the chapter "Beauty and the Beast" that much of this confusion stems from the failure to understand the nature and function of creative art, which Storr refers to as "intellectual creativity." In truth, the key to great art is intuitive insight and imagination, not the power of aggressive reason or intellect.

All these confusions follow logically from a false evaluation of the alleged "dichotomy of the sexes," an evaluation that was itself rooted in the psychopathology of Weininger. A Jew by birth, Weininger rebelled against the strict orthodoxy of his parents, and he grew up to be both violently anti-Semitic and antimaternal. A series of unhappy experiences with women in his adolescent life led him to renounce all sexuality as nonmoral. He became a Christian convert at the age of twenty, and his tragic end in suicide at the age of twenty-three closed the chapter of what has since become a classic case in psychiatric literature.

Weininger's allegiance to the theology of "male genius" and "male morality" required that only men can conceive the "perfect divinity" and become true individuals, that all else is "animalism" and "species survival." Such an allegiance, which would be better called a sickness, inevitably invents a metaphysical dichotomy between the sexes as well as between prehistory and history, between animal nature and human nature. The unconsummated sky god pathology of Weininger's own alienation from the dynamics of nature, compelled him to deny a morality in women. He regarded all maternal love as nonmoral, a mere biological impulse that humans share with the animals: "Motherhood has as little to do with morality as fatherhood. Motherhood, like sexuality, is not an individual relation; it is not a moral individuality that arises from an inner sense of freedom and personal value . . . the female is amoral."[7] He also believed that the failure of the female to be an ethical being stems from "her nonmoral biological instincts and her failure to live up to the ethical standards of man." This ingenious perversion of truth poses the "nonmorality of nature and woman" as the biological enemy of "moral man." It denies an instinctual morality in nature and also the right of woman to express and live by the ideals of human art, morality, and dignity.

The theology of male intellectual and creative superiority is also at work in the silly theory that women are fundamentally and instinctually divergent and men convergent, that man by nature establishes the rationale of life as pope, philosopher, or prime minister, and that any success enjoyed by the divergent female in creative art must be regarded as a harmless little hobby not to be taken too seriously. Her true social role, if indeed she has one, is to provide sympathy, tolerance, and charm and to act as mother to her husband as well as to her children. In return the husband exploits the role of son and loses his sense of responsibility as a father, leaving the care and education of the children in their most formative years to his wife. Those husbands who are comforted by Robert Ardrey's fiction that family life is alien to wild primate society should consult Jojo, whose "fathering behavior" with infant monkeys will educate them on the nature of their own responsibility as parents.

If one were to compile a list of contemporary and distinguished women in government, education, science, painting, sculpture, music, and literature, the establishment males in the tradition of Otto Weininger would no doubt attribute their creative ability to homosexual tendencies, overlooking that one could press a comparable case for exceptional creative ability in men beginning with Socrates, Jesus, Shakespeare, Schumann, Proust, Tchaikovsky, and so on. The whole case for intellectual and creative superiority in the male is unsupportable, if only because there is no complete male or complete female.

Recent hormone experiments show "female" monkeys behaving like males and vice versa. To say that these experiments produce pathological types and not normal healthy animals integrated in their own culture is true; but they also show that an almost infinite variation in the organization and distribution of the sex hormones already exists in people as individuals and not sex genders. These people are not necessarily excessively male-men or female-women. People possess highly creative drives regardless of some arbitrary sex-identity gender, and it does not follow that their potential for love, gentleness, and humility is diminished because of it. There are many men who have a stronger maternal instinct than their wives. These men are not submissive henpecked husbands, nor are their wives pathologically masculine.

It should be obvious that exceptional ability of any kind can be assessed only on the merits of the individual, not by the classification of sexual types. Sexual differentiation is an impossible criterion for explaining the physiology and psychodynamics of creative ability.

In an earlier chapter I considered a number of factors that gave rise to the social domination of the female in human societies: male inheritance of the stronger physique of the forest primates, strengthening of male cooperation by hunting techniques and organization, greater freedom of movement for the hunters and the increasing biological demands made on women by extended child care, male ownership of the tools and weapons for hunting, a further strengthening of male physique and male dominance by the reservation of energy-producing foods tabooed to women. All these factors gave rise to a division of labor based on sex, a division that perpetuated the dependence of women on men. I also considered in chapter 5 that the psychodynamics of male dominance cannot be explained by biological and economic factors alone. Here, however, I am concerned with the simple fact that the traditional role of the male-female relationship in contemporary society has become obsolete.

It is in any event impossible to assess the creative potential of women during a period of two thousand years of male-dominated history, when the political and economic supremacy of men throughout that period remained virtually unchallenged until the turn of the century. Today we need only look back over the past twenty years to recognize the advances women have made in art, science, and government. There are those who may still argue that women cannot aspire to really great art or creative "genius," but I believe we have reached a period in our history where we can no longer afford either the luxury or the danger of the "genius" who stands head and shoulders above all men. The historical conditions that gave rise to the great dinosaurs of the past no longer exist. Healthy societies will always have a need for great artists and great people, but a traditional "genius" in the context of our period of history could only be a freak, and therefore not a genius, if indeed we must continue to use that absurd word to represent the great ones in art. For this and many other reasons I believe that the age of masculine supremacy is near its end. This may come as a great disappointment to those who crave the magic of genius, the great man of the century, a resurrection of the great sky god who usurped the ancient mother goddess as the creative force of generation.

CHAPTER 15

The Natural and the Supernatural

It will be said by many that I have made a mockery of morality by reducing it to a utilitarian ethic. But what moral action would be truly moral if it were not at the same time useful? I agree that he who resists the impulses of his personal advantages and performs sacrifices of every kind is no less "self-indulgent" than the sinner who pursues his advantage. But with this difference: he who is guided by a natural and not a supernatural morality will endeavor to regulate his deeds and his thoughts by a moral imperative that is caressed with life, not the absolutism of a transcendental faith.

Certainly my friend Jojo is guided by his own nature, and he has a conviction about the future, though not a heavenly future in which monkeys will never climb. He also has a hard time fulfilling his obligation to act with a sense of responsibility to others in his colony. Although the church is unlikely to be embarrassed by Jojo's behavior as evidence for a biological morality, it must at least credit Neanderthaler with a soul, since he was reclassified as a true representative of the human race by primatologists in 1957. Neanderthaler made flake tools, a flint-tipped spear, hunted the rhinoceros, and taught his skills to his children. He buried the bodies and the bones of his dead and surrounded them with red ocher, the color of life. If he sought a magic control of the mysterious processes of birth and generation and worshiped his ancestral spirits, it was not because of his need to believe in spiritual perfection, but because he had the natural man's belief in the immortality of life. The popular conception of Neanderthaler as a stooping slant-browed brute who clubbed his woman and dragged her into a cave is convenient for a Christian ideology determined that the iron curtain between prehistory and history should not be lifted. But if we were to equip Neanderthaler with a bowler hat and an umbrella, I am sure he could join the congregation at any church without giving the slightest offense to anyone.

I considered earlier how the concept of the universal has no reality outside the intuitions of our own conscience and our own will. So true is this that we often find a more profound elevation of the soul in the exhortations of the romantic who rebels against the tyranny of an abstract morality. When the poet-philosopher Jacobi was confronted with the choice between a baptized virtue and the passions of the pagan, he cried: "If I must keep to one of these classes I choose the second . . . . Yes, I am impious, I will to break laws like Epaminondes; to despoil the temple like David, to pluck ears of corn on the Sabbath, if only because I am hungry and the law was made for man and not man for the law. By the sacrosanct conscience that I have within me I know that the privilege to desecrate the pure letter of the rational Absolute is the sovereign right of man himself, the seal of his dignity and of his divine nature."

The moral beauty of Jacobi's protest stemmed from his passionate refusal to be suffocated by an abstract universal. His appeal to the truth within the individual was in fact an affirmation of a moral imperative that works instinctually and unmysteriously within the passionate action of the individual. His affirmation was not supposed to provide us with a rigorous philosophy of morality. It was a protest against a dead concept. Jacobi refused to be trapped in the metaphysic of a spurious humility.

There are two main forms of a false humility that work with deadly effect in contemporary religion, one Eastern and the other Western. Institutionalized Christianity subdues the flock with a puritanical morality, while Buddhism sedates its subjects with spiritual apathy. Both are sublime forms of what I call a despotic humilitarianism.

The focal point in Buddhism is to meditate on the "I" as a fragment of the universal and to surrender the concept of individual responsibility to "the subconscious stream of the nonself." This "meditation," which is actually a sublime form of bingo, is understandable in a people who have suffered the poverty of a bare existence and of enslavement by eastern potentates over thousands of years; and we would not expect eastern societies (until they are proletarianized) to exhibit the anticlerical violence found in the West, any more than we would look for it in amoeba communities. It is true that the Christian concept of "identity in a universal God" (which would be better called an indemnity) is abnegated in the eastern conception of an impersonalized divinity and that this total surrender expels the obsessional neuroses of the split mind. Unfortunately it expels the mind as well. In all its historical and social implications the consequence of such an absolute surrender is to destroy a natural sense of responsibility to others at its phylogenetic roots. Speaking for nature, Jojo's inbuilt sense of moral responsibility will force him to fight a predatory eagle to save the infant Polly with a total disregard for "the subconscious stream of the nonself."

In his own way the Buddhist does establish a self-identity with the universe, but he corrupts this identity by treating the universe or nature as though it were an alien subject that does not assert itself with moral force. The concept of force is buried in the abstraction "the universal energy system."[1] The operative word missing is, of course, *responsibility*. A "total cosmic energizing system" begs a "total responsibility," and it is precisely this inbuilt sense of responsibility both to assert and appease (which incidentally characterizes the ecology of nature) that frightens the mystic. He wants no part of it. He escapes by surrendering his own truth to the abstraction "the whole truth," as though an identity with beauty, for example, depended upon a total grasp of all the phenomena of beauty! The confusion feeds on itself, so that the "conceptual ego," overawed by the logical impossibility of thinking and experiencing everything, collapses into a false reverence for a totalizing concept. This leads the Buddhist by the nose to a false humility. He believes that because the individual cannot know the Whole or the All, he must submerge his finite ego in the Infinite and deny the impulse to assert his own will. It is really a philosophy of total appeasement. As Jacobi well knew, the inner gods of wrath take their vengeance on such tomfoolery.

A dialectic conception of evolution informs us that we, like nature, must also act with authority. In this way we oppose nature only to the extent that we stand opposed to ourselves. Freedom and creation do not make sense in any other context. I, for example, stand opposed to the Buddhist conception of nature and the universe, but because Buddhism is also a dimension of the universe and therefore of myself, I oppose myself whenever I am tempted to think and to act like a Buddhist.

The moral arbiter of institutionalized Christianity is also an alien god, one who commands spiritual allegiance to a purity that transcends earthly passion and desire, a god who puts Heaven before earth with the promise of ultimate reconciliation in a Hereafter, and all this despite the argument of the apologists who bleat: the kingdom of God is within. The original notion of reality, worship, and kinship that characterizes tribal religion is reduced by the Christian Church to a theological faith, to an abstract love that sedates the impulse to live with a kind of spiritual onanism. Faith in tribal religion is not an abstraction, but a concrete affinity with nature and history. Our spiritual and biological affinity with nature is impressively symbolized in the Hako ritual of the "pregnant child," in which a child of unidentified sex is affined with the supreme spirit *Tirawa* of nature: "The child is raised in a robe with his legs projecting forward, and in this position he is handled in the fashion of a phallus for a symbolic coitus with the world, represented by a circle outlined on the ground."[2]

Philosophy in our own time affirms man's natural affinity with nature and history and in so doing declares its own universality. This affirmation springs not from a total absence of humility, but from the deducible conviction that the duty and the responsibility of men is not merely to think and act out their "universality" in a monastery, but to transform it into a socialized freedom and justice for people, especially for those who are still alive. In reply to the metaphysic of an "ultimate" triumph of love in a Hereafter, the dialectic philosopher will say: the creation of liberty through struggle in history has and must always be a continuous suffering of love over enmity and of victory over inhumanity.

During a discussion on the possibility of animals surviving in a Hereafter, the missionary in E. M. Forster's *A Passage to India* found himself involved in the argument for a group soul. When he was asked about wasps, cactuses, oranges, crystals, and mud, he quickly changed the subject. The problem of where precisely individuality ends among the animal species is, of course, insoluble. Certainly the higher mammals command our respect as true individuals. Religious people, however, who find the concept of the group soul more attractive, should ask themselves how they would feel if they arrived in Heaven with the hope of meeting a "departed friend" only to be palmed off with an average specimen of the human race. Similarly, if I personally am going to be imprisoned in a Hereafter I shall want to meet my old friend Jojo, not a prototype of *Lagothrix lagotricha*. I am not interested in Jojo's group soul nor in an ideal representative of his species. Monkeys, like humans, behave differently. They are individuals, and one cannot shake hands with a concept.

In all fairness, at least the case for a divine love that embraces all creatures is preferable to the sentiments of those who believe that love should be confined to members of our own "race." Perhaps they can tell us where we should draw the line. With the Tasmanian aborigine, with Cro-Magnon man, Neanderthaler, *Zinjanthropus*, the gorilla, the monkey, the otter, the dog? Who can fix it, and where? All we can say is that when our thoughts rest on such creatures as the moth and the ant, a personal relationship seems absurd. This is not to say that these creatures, which belong to nature no less than we do, are inferior to ourselves and unworthy of admiration; for when we turn from the higher mammals with their marked individuality to the mole, the frog, and to the worms in the earth, love and compassion seem to melt away into a profound reverence for nature in general.

Perhaps the problem of who has a soul and whom we should love is best left as a dilemma for the priest. "Love thy neighbor" was practiced by Paleolithic man in the year 70,000 B.C., but he did not practice a divine and unconditional law of "Love thine enemy." He may have been too fond of his children to take such a risk. As a symbol of peace and goodwill to all men, the negative love of not hating under all circumstances is best done in a monastery, where there are no children. Was the pope who refused to hate and condemn Hitler a more righteous man than the Frenchman or the Englishman who fought and died in the Spanish Civil War knowing that they were fighting the fascism of Franco, Mussolini, and Hitler? The virtue of "Love thine enemy" is highly commendable as a principle that reflects the wisdom of tolerance, appeasement, and forgiveness, but we should think long and hard before inflicting the consequences of its unconditional practice on our children. The Catholic priest will tell us that we may hate the reality of evil as a malignant force, but that evildoers themselves we must love, or learn to love, because like ourselves they are also children of God. The folly of this false humility is apparent to anyone who knows that he must from time to time hate himself, as he must also hate those who strive for ends he earnestly believes to be evil. Motivations do not grow on trees; they are products of people's minds and hearts. The kindness and love we feel for others would not be possible unless we acted on the hatred we have for those who seek power and dominance over the weak and pursue this for its own sake.

Everybody interprets the philosophy of Jesus in his own way. In modern language "Love thine enemy," for me, means no more than that you must first try to placate your enemy, when you may well discover he is not your enemy, but your neighbor. I understand the appeal by Jesus to the virtue of forgiving as a condemnation of the pathological vanity of hating unconditionally all those who think, feel, and act differently to ourselves. To be unforgiving in all circumstances is a crime against humanity. But to be forgiving in all circumstances is to be an insidious vegetating fool. Iroquois Indians adopted captives of war as brothers in their clan. In their savage innocence they would have found the ideals of apartheid incomprehensible. The Eskimo who considers it an honor to have a visiting friend copulate with his wife would regard the racist as a dehumanized idiot. "Judge not lest ye be judged" is a warning, not a taboo on judgment. Taken as the latter, it is an affrontery to the nature and dignity of the human animal, whose inalienable right it is to judge both himself and others and also to be judged by them. The establishment theologian, however, must crush spontaneity at its roots. If you are a good nondissenting Christian you will kneel down with a dead child in your arms and offer the other cheek to those who threw the bomb. And if you are really bighearted you will remember that a hierarchy of politicians, generals, and bishops ordered them to do so in the name of Christian democracy, and you will pray, if you are stark raving mad, "Forgive them, Father, they know not what they do."

There is little doubt that the man Jesus was among the first to resolve the dialectic of love and hate. His supreme task was to reach beyond the chauvinism of a demanding and jealous mother type and beyond the equally chauvinistic and aggressive pack loyalty of the hunting primate. Three times in the Scriptures he protested against the pathological Logos with his own natural aggression: "Ye vipers and whited sepulchres . . . ." His contribution to dialectic philosophy was the principle of uniting two opposing forms of love, each disquiet with its own pathology, into a universal brotherhood of man and woman that united the aggressive ego with the vegetating mother earth: "When you make the male and the female into one—then will you become a living spirit."[3] At the slightest hint of maternal pride, even when couched in praise, he was quick to admonish and warn. A woman said to him: "Blessed is the womb which bore thee and the breasts which nourished thee," and he replied: "The day will come when you will say:

'Blessed is the womb which has not conceived and the breasts which have not suckled.' "[14] Everywhere his concepts emphasize the Here and the Now, and not an expectant future. To the question "Tell us Master, what will the End be?" he replied: "What! Know you the Beginning that you would ask of the End?"[5] In reply to "When will the Kingdom come?" he said: "It will not come by expectation. The kingdom is here, spread upon the earth, but men do not see it."[6] His philosophy rejects holus-bolus the power of an evil environment to defile a good man. As a dialectic principle of self-determination it would be difficult to improve on the following: "Do you not see that there is nothing external to a man which by going into him can defile him? It is the evil thoughts that come from within, out from the heart of man—murder, greed, envy, and folly—that do defile him."[7]

The warnings from Jesus concerning the fate of those who would claim to follow his philosophy exactly and his prediction of the rise of a universal priesthood that would speak in his name and manipulate his philosophy to suit their own ends has clearly come to pass. To the question why has the Chruch survived for nearly two thousand years, one can only say that this malignant wink in the eye of evolution has proved itself a more effective confidence trick than any other for corrupting the theme of man. It also reminds us that the deception we abhor is in ourselves and that a true and natural faith can never be consummated in a yearning for paradise or a distant utopia on earth, or in poetic visions and meditations on the dialectics of love and cruelty, but in a future that is always Here and always Now in the struggle for justice and in the art of being natural.

Notes

Chapter 1   The Innate Drive

1. John Hurell Crook, *Man and Aggression* (London: Oxford University Press, 1968), p. 151.
2. A. C. Hardy, *The Living Stream* (London: Collins, 1965), p. 172.
3. Ashley Montagu, *Culture and the Evolution of Man* (London: Oxford University Press, 1967).
4. Charles Darwin, *The Descent of Man* (London: John Murray, 1890), p. 109.

Chapter 2   Design and Purpose

1. Charles Darwin, *The Variations of Animals and Plants under Domestication* (London, 1868), 2:297.
2. C. H. Waddington, *The Listener Magazine*, November 13, 1952.
3. F. Wood Jones, *Habit and Heritage* (London: Kegan Paul, 1943), p. 99.
4. Ibid., pp. 45–50.
5. L. von Bertalanffy, *The Problems of Life* (New York, 1952), p. 105.
6. F. Wood Jones, *The Matrix of the Mind* (London: Kegan Paul, 1929), p. 27.

Chapter 3   To Humanize or Not

1. Erik H. Erikson, *Insight and Responsibility* (New York: Norton, 1964), p. 229.
2. Oskar Eberle, *Tanz & Theatre der Urvolker* (Freiburg, Olten, 1955).

Chapter 5   The Birth of Sin

1. C. Gale, letter to the author.
2. Leonard Williams, *Samba and the Monkey Mind* (London: Bodley Head, 1965), p. 133.
3. *Human Evolution: Readings in Physical Anthropology*, ed. Noel Korn and Fred Thompson (New York: Holt, Rinehart & Winston, 1967), pp. 174–210.
4. C. R. Carpenter, *Human Evolution: Readings in Physical Anthropology*, ed. Noel Korn and Fred Thompson (New York: Holt, Rinehart & Winston, 1967), p. 194.
5. Claude Lévi-Strauss, *Structural Anthropology* (London: Allen Lane, 1968), p. 259.
6. R. F. Fortune, *Columbia University Anthropology* 14(1932).
7. P. B. Borcherds, *Memoirs* (Cape Town, 1861), p. 114.
8. Marius Schneider, *New Oxford History of Music* (London: Oxford University Press, 1957), 1:10–11.
9. Colin M. Turnbull, *The Forest People* (New York: Simon & Schuster, 1962), p. 154.

Chapter 6   From Hominoid to Hominid

1. Carlton S. Coon, *The Origin of Races* (London: Cape, 1963), pp. 211–215.
2. Ibid., p. 380.
3. Ibid., p. 250.
4. E. O. James, *Prehistoric Religion* (London: Thames & Hudson, 1957), p. 20.
5. Ibid., p. 13.
6. Coon, *Origin of Races*, p. 226.

Chapter 7   The Biocultural Miracle

1. Clifford Geertz, *Human Evolution: Readings in Physical Anthropology*, ed. Noel Korn and Fred Thompson (New York: Holt, Rinehart & Winston, 1967), p. 113.
2. Ibid., p. 117.
3. David A. Hamburg, *Expressions of Emotions in Man* (New York: International Universities, 1963).
4. M. Sahlins, quoted in *Human Evolution*, ed. Korn and Thompson, p. 420.

Chapter 8   The Smile of Hope

1. Erik H. Erikson, *Insight and Responsibility* (New York: Norton, 1964), p. 231.

Chapter 9   Instinct for Continuity

1. P. R. Kirby, *Musical Instruments of Native Races of South Africa* (London: Oxford University Press, 1934), pp. 119–120.
2. Iris Andreski, *Life Stories from Ibibio-land* (London: Routledge & Kegan Paul, 1970).
3. Arthur Koestler, *The Act of Creation* (London: Hutchinson, 1964), p. 168.
4. Franz Boas, *Handbook of American Indian Languages*, part 1, bulletin 40 (1911).
5. Claude Lévi-Strauss, *The Savage Mind* (London: Weidenfeld & Nicolson, 1966), p. 2.
6. W. Barbrook Grubb, *An Unknown People* (London: Seeley, 1911), pp. 319–326.
7. Franz Boas, *The Kwakiutl Indians* (Washington, D.C.: Smithsonian Institute, 1897), pp. 528–529.
8. Leonard Williams, *Study of the Origins of Primitive Music* (London: André Deutsch Ltd., 1967), p. 51.
9. C. Myers, cited in Florence Densmore, *Chippewa Music* (Washington, D.C.: Smithsonian Institution, 1913), p. 13.
10. Ibid., p. 14.
11. G. Turner, *Samoa a Hundred Years Ago* (London, 1884), p. 6.
12. A. H. Smith, *The Culture of the Kabira* (Philadelphia: American Philosophical Society, 1960), p. 150.
13. C. H. Berndt, *Djanggawul* (Melbourne, 1952).
14. Trevor A. Jones, "Arnhem Land Music," *Oceania* 27 (1948).
15. W. B. Grubb, *An Unknown People* (London: Seeley, 1911), p. 111.
16. David St. Clair, *The Mighty Amazon* (London: Souvenir Press, 1968), p. 31.
17. Quentin Crewe, *Sunday Mirror* (London), March 9, 1969.
18. T. G. Strehlow, *Aranda Traditions* (Melbourne, 1947).

Chapter 10   Beauty and the Beast

1. Alexander Humboldt, *Equinoctial Regions of America* 2(1852):414.
2. Franz Boas, *The Kwakiutl Indians* (Washington, D.C.: Smithsonian Institute, 1897), pp. 441–495.
3. Ibid.
4. E. MacCurdy, *Notebooks of Leonardo da Vinci* (London: Cape, 1939), p. 56.
5. Ibid.
6. Iwan Bloch, *Sex Life in England* (London: Francis Aldor, 1938), p. 461.
7. Robert Eisler, *Man into Wolf* (London: Spring Books, 1949), p. 42.
8. S. L. Wasburn, *The Evolution of Hunting* (New York: Holt, Rhinehart & Winston, 1967), p. 67.
9. Laurens van der Post, *The Lost World of the Kalahari* (London: Hogarth Press, 1961), p. 27.

10. Arthur Guirdham, *A Theory of Disease* (London: Allen and Unwin, 1957), p. 63.
11. Claude Lévi-Strauss, *The Savage Mind* (London: Weidenfeld & Nicolson, 1966), p. 105.
12. C. H. Waddington, review of *The Double Helix*, *Times* (London), May 26, 1968).
13. Anthony Storr, *Human Aggression* (London: Penguin, 1968), p. 88.
14. J. Loewenberg, *Hegel* (New York: Scribner, 1929), pp. 378–379.
15. Carl Jung, *Psychology and Religion* (New Haven: Yale University Press, 1944), p. 61.
16. Erik H. Erikson, *Insight and Responsibility* (New York: Norton, 1964), p. 230.
17. Jung, *Psychology and Religion*, pp. 53–54.

Chapter 11   The Great Amoralist

1. Arthur Guirdham, *A Theory of Disease* (London: Allen and Unwin, 1957), p. 197.
2. Robert Eisler, *Man into Wolf* (London: Spring Books, 1949), p. 263.
3. Paul Maclean, quoted in Arthur Koestler, *The Ghost in the Machine* (London: Hutchinson, 1967), p. 287.
4. Erik H. Erikson, *Insight and Responsibility* (New York: Norton, 1964), p. 147.
5. G. W. F. Hegel, *Hegel Selections*, ed. J. Loewenberg (New York: Scribner, Sons, 1929), p. 228.
6. B. Croce, *Philosophy of the Practical* (London: Macmillan, 1913), p. 203.
7. G. W. F. Hegel, *The Logic*, trans. William Wallace (London: Clarendon, 1892), p. 57.
8. H. Rauschnigg, *Hitler Speaks* (London: Butterworth, 1939), p. 247.
9. L. S. Penrose, *Objective Study of Crowd Behavior* (London: Lewis & Co. Ltd., 1952), p. 63.

Chapter 12   Monogamy and Evolution

1. Claude Lévi-Strauss, *Structural Anthropology* (London: Penguin, 1968), p. 340.
2. Karl Marx and Friedrich Engels, *Selected Works* (London: Lawrence & Wishart Ltd., 1953), 2:156.
3. Claude Lévi-Strauss, cited in Marx and Engels, *Selected Works*, 2:345.
4. Ibid., p. 339.
5. Marx and Engels, *Selected Works*, p. 181.
6. Ibid., p. 140.
7. Ibid., p. 178.
8. George B. Schaller, *Year of the Gorilla* (London: Collins, 1965), pp. 37–38.

9. Ibid.
10. Thomas C. Hutchinson, *Science* 158(1967):1467–1470.
11. C. R. Carpenter, "Field Study of the Gibbon," *Com. Psychol. Mono.* 16,5(1940).
12. Leonard Williams, *Man and Monkey* (London: André Deutsch Ltd., 1967), pp. 78–80.
13. C. R. Carpenter, "Field Study of Howler Monkeys," *Com. Psychol. Mono.* 12(1934).
14. Iris Andreski, letters to the author, 1970.
15. Carlton S. Coon, *The Origin of Races* (London: Cape, 1963), p. 102.
16. A. Lommel, *Oceania* 15(1948).

Chapter 13   The Group Family

1. E. O. James, *Prehistoric Religion* (London: Thames & Hudson, 1957), p. 239.
2. Josef Augusta, *Prehistoric Man* (London: Paul Hamlyn, 1964), p. 32.
3. James, *Prehistoric Religion*, p. 164.
4. Ibid., p. 197.
5. Ibid., p. 219.
6. Iris Andreski, *Tribal Woman* (London: Routledge & Kegan Paul, 1970), p. 58.
7. Karl Marx and Friedrich Engels, *Selected Works* (London: Lawrence & Wishart Ltd., 1953), 2:204.
8. Ibid., p. 199.
9. Ibid., p. 201.
10. Marx and Engels, *Selected Works*, 2:208.
11. Ibid.
12. R. D. Laing, *The Politics of Experience* (New York: Penguin, 1967), p. 55.
13. Lewis H. Morgan, *Ancient Society* (London: Macmillan, 1877), p. 552.

Chapter 14   The Sky God

1. W. M. Morton, *Foibles of Insects and Men* (New York, 1928), p. 162.
2. Claude Lévi-Strauss, *Structural Anthropology* (London: Allen Lane, 1968), p. 204.
3. Colin M. Turnbull, *The Forest People* (New York: Simon & Schuster, 1962), p. 164.
4. Otto Weininger, *Sex and Character* (London: Heinemann, 1910), p. 218.
5. Anthony Storr, *Human Aggression* (London: Penguin, 1968), p. 62.
6. Ibid., p. 65.
7. Weininger, *Sex and Character*, p. 214.

Chapter 15 The Natural and the Supernatural

1. Alan W. Watts, *Alternatives to Violence* (New York: Time-Life Books, 1968), p. 112.
2. Claude Lévi-Strauss, *Structural Anthropology* (London: Allen Lane, 1968), p. 238.
3. *Gospel according to Thomas* (London: Collins, 1959), Log. 22, p. 16 and Log. 114, p. 57.
4. Ibid., Log. 77, pp. 43–45.
5. Ibid., Log. 17, p. 13.
6. Ibid., Log. 114, p. 57.
7. *Gospel according to Mark* (London: Marshall & Son, 1904), Log. 7, p. 18.